"The talking points for my calls to the allies need to be on my desk in two hours and the text for tonight's address in four. Take care of getting everything pre-empted; I need to be on every medium where people will have their eyes glued tonight."

"Yes, sir," she replied.

"And Rachel, work with Dr. Holt on everything. I want him read in on every detail."

Chris had been only half-listening until he heard his name. He craned his neck forward and cocked his head to make sure he heard correctly.

"You heard me, Dr. Holt. I need your expertise and as of this moment, you're cleared at the highest possible level and will be given access to any asset the United States government has available that can help us learn more about our visitors before you get out there to meet them in person."

Did he just say I'd be going out there to meet them?

"Sounds like your lucky day."

BAEN BOOKS BY LES JOHNSON

❋ ❋ ❋

with Ben Bova
Rescue Mode

with Travis S. Taylor
Back to the Moon
On to the Asteroid

Edited by Les Johnson and Jack McDevitt
Going Interstellar

**Edited by Les Johnson and
Robert E. Hampson**
Stellaris: People of the Stars (forthcoming)

MISSION TO METHONE

LES JOHNSON

BAEN

MISSION TO METHONE

A Baen Books Original

Baen Publishing Enterprises
P.O. Box 1403
Riverdale, NY 10471
www.baen.com

ISBN: 978-1-4814-8388-9
Cover art by Bob Eggleton

First printing, February 2018
First mass market printing, March 2019

Library of Congress Control Number: 2017052469

Distributed by Simon & Schuster
1230 Avenue of the Americas
New York, NY 10020

10 9 8 7 6 5 4 3 2 1

MISSION TO METHONE

PROLOGUE

The energy released in the first impact was an impressive 4,000,000,000,000,000 joules, the equivalent of about a million tons of TNT, or about enough energy to power the modern United States for a few days. Had the impact happened in the twenty-first century, it would have been an exciting day for the world's astronomers. Instead, the only observers were groups of nomads in the deserts of North Africa and Central Asia, who happened to be under clear skies and in the Earth's shadow. What they saw was a brief flash coming from the Moon, which would have been mostly ignored as if they were seeing things had it not been followed in quick succession by five more flashes, each producing approximately the same energy as the first. Legends were born that night on Earth, legends of gods building huge fires upon the Moon to show their displeasure with the ways of men. On the Moon, it was definitely a scene of anger unleashed. Anger older than humanity was being rained upon a newly established base there.

Keeper-of-the-Way survived the first impact, as did most of her fifty-one crew members. They knew the attack was coming, they just didn't know when—until about twenty terrestrial days before when their telescopes spotted the incoming asteroid swarm headed their way. Had it been one one-hundred-foot-diameter asteroid coming toward the Moon, the Observers in the lunar base might have thought it to be an unlucky coincidence of nature and dispatched one of their kinetic interceptors to deflect it. But it wasn't alone. A sequence of twenty-five similar sized asteroids were coming out of the glare of the Sun with predicted impact points within a few miles of each other—all on Earth's moon and near their base. This was not an act of nature; it was an act of war.

The Observers launched their limited supply of interceptors, propelled by compact matter/antimatter drives capable of accelerating them to nearly ten percent of the speed of light. At impact, each antimatter interceptor released approximately fifty megatons of TNT equivalent energy, enough to deflect the asteroid away from the base toward impact elsewhere on the Moon. They had only twenty interceptors . . .

Keeper-of-the-Way moved quickly, using her three squid-like tentacles to pull herself across the moist floor toward the control panel from which she could determine the full extent of the damage to her base. From the control panel display, she determined that devastation following the first impact was crippling, but not fatal to the Observers' outpost. The damage was restricted to the new construction on the equatorial side of the base, leaving much of the control station and habitat untouched. The atmospheric generators were functioning as were the water-effusing systems. *Good*, she thought to herself, *we won't yet suffocate or desiccate. But for how long?* She knew that more impacts were coming, and unless a miracle occurred, death would soon be upon them all.

Keeper-of-the-Way was startled by Defender-of-All's reedy voice beside her. She hadn't noticed his sliding approach until he spoke. "We will not survive much longer. The battle in the outer system must have been lost or the Bringers-of-Death would not be able to mount such a strike."

"I fear you are correct," she said with great sadness. She so wanted to see the star of Homeworld again from the shores of the lake in which she spawned. That, and she feared that the species they were sent here to observe would be destroyed by the Bringers-of-Death before they had the opportunity to hatch into their own as an advanced civilization and technological society. "Is there nothing more that we can do?"

"Nothing. We used all the interceptors we have available. If the supply ships hadn't been caught amongst the fleet battle near the ringed planet, then we might have had a chance."

Keeper-of-the-Way looked at the radar return showing the imminent impact of the next asteroid, took Defender-of-All's middle manipulator tentacle into her own, performed the ceremonial clutching of suckers, and bowed her head.

Defender-of-All returned the clutching and also bowed his head.

Fifteen seconds later, the second asteroid struck the command center and vaporized it and all within. Before twenty minutes had passed, there were several new craters on the lunar surface where the base had once stood. Pieces of the base, the Moon, and the impacting asteroid gained enough energy from the collision to escape the pull of the Moon's gravity and fly off into space. Some flew toward the Earth and caused a spectacular meteor shower visible only to those residing in the northern part of Asia at the time. Other pieces entered a low lunar orbit and remained there for almost a year before the asymmetric tug of the lunar gravity field caused them to spiral in and impact the Moon themselves. Still others were kicked all the way around the Moon and managed to fly back to almost their point of ejection, causing only minor additional damage from what was, by any means measurable, a catastrophic attack from which there were no survivors.

It was a scene that had been played out for millennia across numerous stellar systems, on or near numerous worlds with indigenous life, and had determined the fate of intelligent, tool-using species too numerous to count.

On Earth's moon, there remained almost no trace of the alien base that had once resided there.

CHAPTER 1

Space exploration was months of boredom punctuated by moments of extreme excitement and discovery, or at least that's how it seemed to Chris Holt as he poured over the morning flight data reports for the five spacecraft he was responsible for keeping alive and functioning. From his windowless office at Space Resources Corporation, he couldn't even have the thrill of seeing the rain squalls pummeling the Gulf Coast from yet another tropical depression in the Gulf of Mexico. He was still wet after making a mad dash from his Personal Transportation Vehicle to his office nearly two hours ago.

Using his 'net goggles to review the reports, he intently read the ghostly status results as they slid into and out of view on his personal heads-up display, obscuring his "real" view of the wall in front of his desk. Chris hadn't yet opted for the newly-released cornea implants that were quickly making goggles obsolete. He wanted them to be out for at least a few years before he let anyone implant them in *his* eyes.

The reports, which were created overnight by the lab's artificial intelligence, affectionately known as SNARC by the engineers, were full of the flight data from each of the spacecraft's primary subsystems.

Chris was mainly interested in how the solar sails that propelled the small spacecraft through space were performing and whether or not anything needed to be done to adjust their trajectories to assure each would arrive at the designated asteroid at the right time. The data collected would help provide Space Resources Corporation with the information it needed to determine which asteroids would be good candidates for follow-up exploration and mining. Lots of money was at stake, and Chris was the one responsible for making sure that the mining engineers got the data they needed to advise the company's president and board of directors where to go next.

Using solar sails to propel the company's fleet of reconnaissance spacecraft had been his idea, and, so far, it appeared to have been a good investment. Each robotic spacecraft was barely larger than a shoebox, carried a camera and spectrometer to gather the asteroid data needed for assay, and was propelled by reflecting sunlight from a one-thousand-square-foot sail made of a reflective film thinner than a human hair. Without the need for fuel, and the only visiting asteroids closer to the Sun than Mars, solar sail propelled spacecraft never ran out of fuel and could operate as long as the sun was shining. But they were slow to accelerate and would require between one and three years after launch to reach their targets.

Now one of them was getting close to its rendezvous. Chris knew that the first usable photos should be coming in as early as today. The photos taken by the ship's onboard camera so far were as expected: they showed a bright dot, taking up no more than a few pixels, growing larger with each passing day. The image processing team already had enough data to give him an indication of the asteroid's overall shape and rotation rate. Asteroid 2055VG, named for the year it was discovered, was shaping up to be interesting indeed. The initial data showed that it wasn't rotating and that it appeared to be almost spherical—making it an oddity among asteroids, which were usually elliptical and irregular, not round. He was looking forward to honest-to-God photos taken up close and personal from about one hundred feet away, which would be in his hands by the end of the week or sooner.

Four of the five spacecraft were operating normally, constantly and ever-so-slightly varying their trajectories through space to allow them to rendezvous with their designated asteroids at the right time—after maneuvering tens, and in some cases, hundreds of millions of miles since departing Earth. One was not operating as planned. Chris saw that the problem with the spacecraft was first reported during the night shift just before his arrival. Also included in the data were spacecraft temperature measurements, solar array power output stats, and a plethora of data that would only make sense to the various subsystem engineers who were periodically reviewing the data and responding to anomaly reports like the one that Chris had just found for AB-22.

He saw that the overnight staffer overrode one of the automated command uplinks that would have adjusted the trajectory of spacecraft AB-22 to account for an unexpected drop in overall thrust.

"The idiot didn't even follow up by checking the context camera," he mumbled to himself as he accessed the data streaming down from AB-22 in search of the spacecraft's most recent self-shot. After a few moments, he found the data set containing the picture library and was looking at the distorted fish-eye view of the spacecraft's solar sail.

"Shit."

Chris activated the communications link embedded in his right cheek, and called his chief engineer, Pam Stark.

"Pam, AB-22 has a small tear in quadrant four. Yesterday's data showed a change in the sail's thrust level and a shift in its center of pressure. The idiot on the night shift got the flag and didn't even try to see what was causing the problem. He just uploaded a new trajectory model and went back to playing a video game or whatever else he could waste time with instead of working. We need to update the sail's thrust model and probably increase the spin rate to compensate for the extra torque. If we keep adjusting the trajectory, it'll cause a huge increase in flight time."

"I'm on it. Mattias was on shift last night, wasn't he?"

"I think so. Do you want to talk to him or do you want me to?"

"I'd better do it," she replied.

"Good. I'm so angry I can't see straight."

"I'm on it," she said, cutting the connection.

Chris was so engaged with reviewing the data coming through his 'net goggles that he didn't hear Vasilisa open the door and halfway enter his office until she spoke, startling him. Sometimes it was difficult to separate what was real from what came through the 'net.

"Chris, are you still interested in lunch?"

Vasilisa was Space Resources Corporation's Vice President for Mining Operations, overseeing nearly two billion dollars of the company's interplanetary mining investments. She was originally from Russia, but had become totally Americanized by forty years of living in the United States. Chris had many times heard her horrific story of surviving the nuclear blast that had leveled most of the South Korean city of Daejeon while she was a graduate student there. She mentioned many times how her life would have been different had she decided to pursue her graduate studies in Moscow instead of Daejeon. For Chris, this was ancient history—having occurred five years before his birth. Like most people, real "history" began with their own awareness of the world. But Chris liked her, and thoroughly enjoyed the rare moments she was available to meet with him for lunch. She understood him like almost no one else and was always there when he needed someone to talk to. Today was one of those days.

"Absolutely! You just surprised me," he replied, rising from behind his meticulously organized desk.

"I'm surprised the 'Net Assistant didn't remind you. Do you have it turned off again?"

"Well, not completely off, but I've silenced all the usual stuff while I review this data. You know how it distracts me."

"Personally, I don't see how any of your generation can

get work done with fully active 'net access. Having all the information in the world scrolling through your field of vision constantly would just drive me crazy."

"That's why I use my 'net goggles with it turned off. Too addictive. I have more important things to do than playing games and watching porn. Besides, it gives me a headache."

"We'd better get moving to the cafeteria or what little time I have for lunch will get swallowed. I've got a VR meeting after lunch."

Chris rose from his chair and joined Vasilisa as they walked down the hall toward the company's cafeteria. The usual aromas of exotic spices wafted into the hallway ahead of their entry into the brightly lit room that fed the company's fifteen hundred employees. Chris was thoroughly accustomed to the extreme diversity of ethnic backgrounds that worked for Space Resources Corporation. The company only recruited the best and brightest from around the world. Vasilisa had related stories of her youth, when extreme intercultural mixing was only just beginning—especially in Russia. Her stories were high on the list of what Chris liked about Vasilisa. That and her uncanny ability to see through the usual political bullshit that people in her class of friends and business associates must deal with on a daily basis. She was a rare "I am what I am" kind of person who wasn't afraid of telling people how she saw things. And it had worked in her favor on many occasions. That was why they liked each other— neither was afraid of calling out mistakes made by others nor would they put up with less than stellar technical performance by any in the office. Their only difference was one of style: Vasilisa was way more tactful in how she communicated than Chris. He knew it and hated it—no matter how hard he tried, his words usually managed to offend someone.

They chose to eat plain, run-of-the-mill Chinese and found a secluded table in the far corner of the room next to one of the large windows that overlooked the company's well-tended garden. The garden looked soggy from being pounded by relentless rain coming from a dark grey, menacing sky.

"Tell me what you've got. I understand one of your babies is close to rendezvous."

"Close. The imaging team gave me some preliminary data already. We might get a good image back as early as this afternoon." Chris was in his element now, and he knew it. He enjoyed his time chatting with Vasilisa; he suspected it was his energy and enthusiasm for his work that she relished.

"When will we have enough information for the Assay Assessment Team?"

"We should be alongside and taking extremely high-resolution photos within the week. If it looks promising, then your division can have at it. If not, then, well, we've done more science and can turn all the data over to the NSF." Even though the company considered the latter case to be a failure, since it wouldn't make them any money, Chris, who was trained as a physicist, was a scientist at heart and didn't mind turning over all the data collected to the National Science Foundation. For Chris, scientific data was as valuable as platinum.

"I saw that gleam in your eye when you mentioned the

NSF. We aren't going to lose you to some university, are we?"

"Not a chance. They can't come close to paying me what you do. Besides, they don't have the money to send spacecraft exploring." Chris smiled as he played on an old theme from conversations past: the need to pay scientists more money to encourage more to go into science and engineering fields. She didn't appear to take the bait.

"Tamika told me you've been invited to speak at the International Astronautical Congress in Sweden. What's your topic?"

"I've built a roadmap for what comes next. With the Moonbase built, Mars being explored and real commerce finally happening in near-Earth space, we're on our way to becoming a solar system-wide civilization. Have you heard about the fusion drive research at Livermore labs? Europa here we come!"

"Chris, do you really want to unleash the Caliphate on the stars? They're living like it's the year 800 and want to drag the rest of us back there with them. What about all of our petty conflicts, not to mention our wars? Somehow I don't believe we'll suddenly stop fighting each other if we go to the stars."

"I don't want the Caliphate to go. But they probably will. They, the Indians, the Chinese and all the rest will go right along with us. Nothing depresses me more than to think of us being stuck forever in the solar system when there is a universe out there waiting to be explored. I think we must go to preserve and spread life. If we stay here, the Caliphate or some virus might wipe us out. We have to go. We just need to convince the idiots with all the money that it needs to happen."

"But do you think it's even possible? Where is everybody? I think we're *it* and we're *stuck*. Just like this shrimp." Vasilisa followed her last point by biting a whole piece of fried shrimp in a particularly dramatic fashion.

"Vasilisa, you just don't think big enough. We're mining asteroids, bringing raw materials back to the Moon and Moonbase, keeping it functioning—at a profit. And you just announced last week that we'll be dropping processed ore into Utah and Nevada and putting it up for sale in the terrestrial market. How can you be so negative?"

"Because I've seen the horrific videos coming out from the Caliphate. I've lived through a nuclear blast that killed over two million people. I've seen the US and China go at each other and almost blast the world back into the Stone Age over a silly little island in the Pacific. I'm negative because even the way I earn my living is based on consuming raw materials from other worlds to make more stuff for people to buy and then eventually put into a garbage dump."

"We need to get out there before the assholes screw it all up to the point that we can never recover and go."

"Well, I think …" Vasilisa began but was interrupted by Chris raising his hand and turning his head away.

"Hold on," he said as he cocked his head, activated the audio implant in his earlobe and listened to the message demanding his attention.

"Chris—the first image from asteroid 2055VG17 is here and it'll knock your socks off. Do you have your 'net goggles on?"

"No, I left the damned things at my desk." Chris's voice was firm but barely audible to anyone near him in the room.

"Okay. Listen up. Get over here as quick as you can. It doesn't just look like a sphere, it is a sphere. Perfectly round. And it looks to be artificial."

"Excuse me, what did you say?" Chris asked, his voice now loud enough for Vasilisa to hear and understand.

"I said, it doesn't look like it's natural. No, it isn't natural. It's clearly artificial."

Chris was out of his chair and moving toward the door before Vasilisa realized he was even moving.

CHAPTER 2

Space Resources CEO Jim Moorman looked impatient and worried. Standing just under six feet tall, Moorman didn't look even close to his biological age—which was seventy-one. Clearly the beneficiary to the best anti-aging treatments his wealth could buy, Moorman looked more like a man in his mid-thirties. His brown hair, only slightly receding, showed not a single sign of grey, and wrinkles were limited to a few minor ones on his forehead. It was those minor wrinkles that now stood out as his patience at not being informed of what his team had discovered was starting to wear thin.

"Okay, what do we know about this thing?" asked Moorman.

"And who have you told about it?" added a voice from Moorman's right. The speaker was Space Resources' Legal Counsel, Tamika Marsee. Chris knew that Marsee was good at her job and he respected that. Even if she sometimes overstepped her authority and tried to assert company control over his publications and speaking engagements, he knew she was just trying to look out for the best interests of the company. He respected her, but he didn't particularly like her.

All eyes turned toward Chris. It was his team that made the discovery using his spacecraft.

"All that you are going to see was prepared by Chandra and me. No one else is in the loop. First of all, we know that it isn't an asteroid. It's clearly artificial. It's what we call an Inner Earth Object, meaning that its aphelion is about zero point nine eight astronomical units. Its closest approach to the Earth's orbit is about point zero two AU, and that only happens once in a dozen years or so. It's shaped like a sphere and almost four hundred feet in diameter. It's black, and from what we can tell, it hasn't been there very long." Chris paused to make sure Moorman was following him.

"Do we know who launched it? China? The Europeans? India?" asked Marsee.

Trying to be patient with those who didn't have the technical background he had, Chris picked up his 'net goggles from the table next to him and put them on like a pair of old fashioned eye glasses. He motioned for others to do the same, which most did. Those who didn't activated their corneal implants. All fifteen people in the conference room were now looking at a very realistic three-dimensional view of what appeared to be a black sphere that was barely discernible against the background of stars. The sun was not in view; it appeared to be behind the viewer, in this case the spacecraft's camera, providing the illumination of the eerie looking ball.

"Take a look at the object and imagine a soccer field next to it. They would be the same size. No nation on

Earth can launch something that large. So, no, the Chinese didn't launch it.

"Now watch it as we get closer. The scout is designed to fly within one hundred feet of its target and that's what we did."

The image in the 'net goggles grew larger and larger until it was no longer possible to see it in its entirety against the backdrop of the stars. Instead, all one could see was a curved surface extending out of the field of view on every side of the viewer that at one time must have been fairly smooth across its length—but not anymore. Instead, the surface was marked by numerous craters and scorch marks.

"The object is mostly smooth but looks to be severely damaged. If I had to hazard a guess, I'd say the ship was at one time a perfect sphere. But it looks like it's taken some pretty heavy damage."

"Could meteors do that?" asked Moorman.

"No. The meteor flux is mostly composed of relatively small particles. They could account for some of the much smaller blotches here and there, but these large craters had to be caused by something a lot more energetic than a micrometeor traveling at eighteen kilometers per second or so. Also, if you look closely in quadrant three, you'll see extreme surface ablation. In my opinion, the ablation was caused by a nuclear weapon."

"You can't be *serious*," exclaimed Marsee.

"Whatever this is, it was savagely attacked by someone, or something, at about the time our ancestors were walking the savannahs in Africa and thinking of moving to other parts of the globe. And that's not all."

"Keep going," said Moorman.

"The object is mostly smooth, but every so often you can see relatively small hemispherical bumps on the surface. God only knows what they are. And, as the camera panned across the surface flying by, we saw this." The goggle image now had an oval highlighted section, visible within the field of view of the camera as a circle with an iris-like pattern within it.

"Is that an . . ." started to ask one of the engineers in the audience.

"It looks like it might be a door or an airlock," replied Chris, cutting the engineer off before he could steal his carefully planned dramatic moment.

"A door?" Moorman cocked his head to the side as he asked the question and peered more closely at the image.

"That's right, but only a guess. Who knows what an alien mind might design into a spacecraft?" Chris replied.

Chris had just acknowledged the elephant in the room and was waiting on some sort of response. It was the moment of the meeting he'd been waiting for.

"Aliens? Space war? And now an airlock? Is this April first and I missed the memo?" The comment was from Jin Gearhart, Chris's long-time, pain-in-the-ass nemesis who seemed to question every decision, request and idea that Chris brought to the table within the company. Gearhart, who had less than half the number of peer reviewed publications as Chris and who had never been written up in the journal Nature, was an *unnecessary* pain in the ass.

"I'm not kidding. We're looking at an alien spacecraft for the first time in human history. First contact. This is a big fucking deal."

The room erupted with conversation. Chris, feeling pleased with himself, took off the 'net goggles and sat them on the table as he first looked around the room at his colleagues, then directly at Gearhart to whom he couldn't help but give a condescending smirk, and finally to Moorman.

Moorman, clearly fully engaged and activating his "CEO personality," took charge.

"Chris, this is amazing news. I want you to capture as much data as you can about the object and put it into a holo-presentation that I can use when the news goes public. I assume the spacecraft is on-station and monitoring it?"

"Not exactly. We flew by at about ten feet per second to take these images and now we're well past it. Remember a solar sail can't really stop. You can't turn off the sun. I've got Julianna working on a return trajectory instead of retargeting to the next asteroid. I haven't filled her in and she thinks we just need more data to complete the assay. We should be back at the target in about two weeks for another slow flyby."

"Tamika, I want to know our legal options and responsibilities. Can we claim it? Is there some sort of space equivalent to the law of the sea that allows us to claim a derelict spacecraft?"

"Yes, sir, there is. But those laws imply that the derelict is a spacecraft launched from Earth. I'm not sure about us legally claiming an alien spaceship that's been adrift for a million years."

"It can't have been there for more than a hundred thousand years or so," Chris interjected.

"How do you know that?" asked Gearhart, looking incredulously at Chris.

"Because the undamaged surface of the ship is still relatively smooth. It hasn't had time to be pockmarked by too many micrometeors and it doesn't have a noticeable layer of dust. It would be much more pitted and dirty if it'd been there for a million years." *And this is so completely obvious.*

Moorman replied, sounding more than a little annoyed, "I don't really care if it's been there for five minutes or fifty million years. I want my property rights respected when we go public with this. Can you imagine the technology behind such a ship? I realize we're likely to lose control over what happens next with this thing, but I won't give up my claims without a lot of noise and, if it comes down to it, a lot of money. Make it happen, Tamika."

"I'll try."

"And one last thing. Keep this quiet. I don't want this to leak to the press or anybody until we have a plan. You all signed NDAs and I expect you to abide by them."

With that, the meeting was adjourned and Moorman walked out. Chris took a deep breath, walked over to Vasilisa and grinned.

"Now you know why I walked out of our lunch date."

CHAPTER 3

It was times like this that Chris wished he had a wife, children, or some sort of family with whom he could share the excitement of what was happening. He was on his way to meet with the president of the United States to talk about how he found an alien artifact and answered one of the oldest questions known to man—are we alone in the universe? Who did he share the news and excitement with? Only his two dogs, Cricket and Panda. They were awake and up with him, barely, as he left his apartment to catch the early flight to Washington. His parents were dead and his sister was off somewhere, God only knew where, with that missionary husband of hers on yet another trip to save the heathens. Sometimes he envied her; she was *living* in a way he could only, barely, imagine. Yes, Chris was successful by just about any measure the world could devise, but sometimes he felt like a complete loser. This morning as he left home and dropped his dogs off (again) at the local dog sitting service, was one of those days.

"Is this your first trip to The White House?" asked the woman in the driver's seat as they approached the gates on the east side of the White House. She wasn't driving; the security system had now taken over controlling the vehicle as it approached the restricted zone that encircled the White House grounds. They were now no longer in control of reaching their final destination and, if Chris Holt guessed correctly, they were being scanned by every sort of remote sensing device imaginable. With the continued existence of the Caliphate, the threat of terrorism was ever present.

Chris Holt looked out the window as the car slowed and approached the gate, barely even acknowledging her latest attempt at polite conversation. They'd been together now for well over two hours and, as far as Chris was concerned, they might never meet again. To him, such a short interaction didn't warrant the effort it would take to engage in small talk. He had talking points to review lest he screw up and say the wrong thing to the president. Besides, engaging in small talk was arduous. He would have to pay attention to not only what she was saying, but to her facial expressions, her body language, and, God help him, her verbal inflections. Why was talking to non-technical people so much harder than tensor calculus? He didn't want to be rude to her, but sometimes it was just easier to be quiet and considered rude than do all the work necessary to talk with someone and *engage* them. *Of course*, he thought, *that's probably why I live alone with my dogs.* But the thought couldn't overcome his reluctance to participate in small talk.

"Humph," she said when she received no response

from him. Melissa Reed was part of the President's Secret Service protection detail, a former US Air Force surrogate pilot, and a very attractive woman. She was clearly not used to being ignored.

A team of inspectors with all sorts of scanning gear approached the car from the gate and proceeded to give it a once-over. Despite all the electronic equipment available, there was also a dog team brought out to sniff. *This* Chris noticed.

"You'd think they'd have better tech and wouldn't need the dogs anymore. I guess you guys are still one step out of date," said Chris, as he tried to not completely ignore her.

"Hardly. There's nothing better than canine olfactory for finding explosives. If you so much as touched an explosive in the last few days, they'll alert on you."

"Really?" That was a claim he would have to research. He made a mental note to look up the status of bomb detection technology when he returned home. This was item number seventeen on his list for the day but it was interesting enough to perhaps move up in priority to somewhere in the top five. He suspected his list would be long after the meeting he was about to attend and briefly wondered if he should actually write any of the list down, but then decided against it. He never forgot such things and there was no reason to expect today would be different than any other day in that regard—meeting with the president, notwithstanding.

The car began moving again and rolled at a leisurely pace as it wound its way around the semicircular drive along the South Lawn and toward the White House. Not even Chris could resist looking out the window as the car took him toward his first-ever meeting with a sitting president. He'd met ex-President Pinto shortly after she'd left office and become the president at Boston University, where he had been working as a post-doc. At the time, he was very impressed. Once he saw how she ran the university after taking over, not so much. She brought in all her crony friends and, at least in Chris's opinion, ruined the graduate programs there. He wasn't holding out much hope that President Kremic was any better.

The car stopped and the door was opened by one of the many dark-suited men and women who seemed to be everywhere he looked. As he lifted himself out and into the brisk morning air, he saw NASA Administrator Fuqua in a small crowd of men and women engaged in a discussion. He'd met Fuqua at conference a few years ago, just after he'd been named administrator. *This* was someone who impressed him.

"Dr. Holt, if you'll follow me please, we need to get you inside." He was greeted by one of the men in dark suits and dark sunglasses who placed his hand on Chris's arm to guide him toward the door.

The other group joined him and, as they walked through the massive doors into the building, they one-by-one introduced themselves and shook hands. Chris wasn't surprised to learn that most were active duty military, General This or General That. His mind was still preoccupied with the Artifact and he didn't allocate the effort it would take to *remember* names.

They didn't waste any time moving down the wood-floored and ostentatiously adorned hallway to a large conference room already filled with at least twenty other people, all looking expectantly toward them as they entered the room.

Chris was guided to the seat adorned with his name on a placard placed between Administrator Fuqua and some other dignitary.

Moments after taking his seat, President Kremic entered the room, escorted by a man and a woman, all of whom looked harried. Chris couldn't help but smirk at what he perceived as their sense of self-importance. In the excitement of the moment, he forgot to hide, or at least mask, the smirk.

Kremic looked in person just as he did on screen and during press conferences. With CGI having replaced most actors these days, Chris half-expected the "real" Kremic to look nothing at all like did in the media.

"Ladies and gentlemen, thank you for coming. Some of you are already aware of the nature of this meeting, most are not, so I will get right to the point. There is an alien spacecraft in our solar system and we need to figure out what to do about it." Kremic was known as a man who didn't beat around the bush.

For the first few moments, no one made a sound. All Chris could hear was his heart beating as he felt his pulse quicken. This was it. His data had undoubtedly been confirmed, as he knew it would be. Then the murmuring began.

"Before we get off track, let me assure you that the information you are about to hear has been reviewed by NASA, the Air Force and the National Security Agency. What's been found is real and may pose an imminent threat to the security of the United States. Next, I'd like to introduce Dr. Chris Holt, the man who discovered what we're calling the Artifact. He's with Space Resources and, from what I understand, he discovered the Artifact with one his of prospecting spacecraft. Dr. Holt, you have the floor."

President Kremic looked at Chris like he'd known him for years as he motioned for Chris to begin his briefing. The fact was, they'd never actually met. Chris had to assume that Kremic has been fully briefed on his background so that he could give such a disingenuous, but accurate, introduction. A politician.

"Thank you, Mr. President. If you will activate your 'net goggles or corneal implants to channel three, I'll walk you through how we found the Artifact and what we know about it. First of all, we discovered it using one of our robotic solar sail prospectors . . ." Chris went through the details of the Artifact's discovery and showed those assembled every significant photo they had taken to date. The briefing took thirty minutes and not a sound could be heard in the room until he finished and asked for questions.

"Dr. Holt. Are you telling us this thing may have been out there for a hundred thousand years? Really?" The question came from one of the suits at the table.

"That's an upper limit based on our observations of the Artifact's surface and the very minor age-related damage it has taken. The size of the dust layer, the pitting from the occasional micrometeoroid strike, and other space environmental effects lead me to believe that it can't possibly have been there for more than a hundred thousand years nor is it likely that it's been there for *less* than ten thousand years. It isn't pristine, but not significantly weathered either."

"I say we nuke it," said another of the suits at the table. Chris couldn't read the man's nametag; he was at the far end of the table, and it was a long table.

"Out of the question. We have too much to learn here and I don't want to be the president who starts a war," said Kremic.

"War with whom?" asked one of the female "suits" who sat on the opposite side of the table from the man who suggested nuking the Artifact.

"War with another, potentially much more advanced technological civilization. War with an alien species that may be as far removed from us as we are from our ancestors on the African savannah," said Chris.

"Aliens? Surely, they're long gone if the Artifact has been out there as long as you say it has," replied the suit.

"I don't know what agency or organization you represent, but your ignorance and ill-informed suggestions are counterproductive," said Chris. He'd had just about enough of bureaucratic morons in his career and having one involved in a discussion of this importance and magnitude was galling. He knew as he said it that he was probably being too blunt, but the words came out before he could contain them. *Shit. I bet I just made an enemy.*

"Dr. Holt, I assure you that . . ."

"Enough!" said the president. "Dr. Holt, do you believe the Artifact might still be inhabited?"

"Mr. President, I don't know if it's inhabited or not, but I do know that whoever sent this ship to our solar system has a perspective on time that dwarfs anything in our experience. Do you know how far away the nearest star system is? Well, I'll tell you. It's over four light years away. You think that's close? It isn't. If you take the Sun-to-Earth distance of ninety-three million miles and shrink that to one foot, then the Earth would be one foot from the Sun and Pluto would be about thirty-eight feet away. On that scale, the nearest star is over fifty miles away. And whatever aliens sent this ship our way probably aren't from the Centauri system—they've come much further. Given what we know about the universe and the laws of physics, this Artifact might have been traveling through deep space for a thousand years before arriving here. Whoever built this thing has to be taking the long view and I would bet that someone or something is out there actively watching us. It certainly *could* be dead, but my money is on the opposite."

"Folks, we need options and we need them fast. This is the kind of thing that leaks and we need to have a plan before I have to address the American people about an alien probe being found."

"Mr. President, we can repurpose the ship we're building for our next Mars mission and send it to this thing instead," said NASA Administrator Fuqua. Fuqua's quick offer to use a NASA resource to visit the Artifact notched him up yet further in Chris's estimation.

"How soon could it be ready to fly?" asked President Kremic.

"Three to five months. We've been making excellent progress and everything is on schedule."

"That's a first," said someone at the table, Chris

couldn't be quite sure who because he hadn't been looking. He was lost in thought about aliens and what their "alien" motivations might be. He'd been worrying about this since the day the Artifact was discovered and grew more worried as he realized humanity was going to attempt to make first contact.

"Get me a brief on what that's going to take technically and budget-wise. I'll need to apprise Congress."

"Yes, sir. And, um, sir, what about our partners? Once we start making changes to the manifest and CONOPS, the Europeans and Japanese are going to start asking questions," said Fuqua.

"I'll deal with our allies. Before we go public with this, I'll personally inform them, the Chinese general secretary and the Indian president, God help me. And once they know, then it'll be only a matter of hours or minutes before the story leaks to every media outlet in the world. Those bastards wouldn't know how to keep something quiet if their lives depended on it. I'll be making the calls later today and addressing the American people tonight."

"Tonight? What if there's panic or something?" asked the suit who suggested nuking the Artifact. Chris could now read his badge and see that he was President Kremic's director of Homeland Security.

"Tonight, Alan. No debate." President Kremic turned to the woman on his right, who Chris knew to be his chief of staff, Rachel Suddoth. She was impeccably dressed in the latest New York fashion and looked to be no more than thirty-five years old. Chris wondered how someone so new to the political scene could be in the room, let alone in such a high position within the administration.

"Rachel, I need you to pull this all together. The talking points for my calls to the allies need to be on my desk in two hours and the text for tonight's address in four. Take care of getting everything pre-empted; I need to be on every medium where people will have their eyes glued tonight."

"Yes, sir," she replied.

"And Rachel, work with Dr. Holt on everything. I want him read in on every detail."

Chris had been only half-listening until he heard his name. He craned his neck forward and cocked his head to make sure he heard correctly.

"You heard me, Dr. Holt. I need your expertise and as of this moment, you're cleared at the highest possible level and will be given access to any asset the United States government has available that can help us learn more about our visitors before you get out there to meet them in person."

Did he just say I'd be going out there to meet them?

"Sounds like your lucky day," said Rachel with a smile.

CHAPTER 4

"Mr. President, this could lead to another war. One that would make the Asian War look like a picnic." Speaking to the president of the United States was his secretary of state, Taimi Gierow. Gierow, a long-time Washington insider, was in the US Senate in 2050 when the tensions in Asia over some obscure islands that both China and Japan claimed as their own came to a head and resulted in a US aircraft carrier being sunk and the first nuclear weapon being used in wartime since over a century before. If the crazy leader in North Korea hadn't taken advantage of a distracted China and USA to attack the south—and drop an atomic bomb on the South Korean city of Daejeon—then either the USA or China might have seriously considered using their own nuclear weapons. But when they saw the horrific images coming out of South Korea, they put their differences about some minor islands aside and instead combined forces to eliminate a very real, credible threat to world peace—North Korea. Today, just fifteen years later, Kremic and

Gierow didn't want to see the strides made since that dreadful day reversed because of the object found in deep space.

President Kremic, seated at his desk in the newly renovated Oval Office, couldn't agree more. Kremic stroked his salt and pepper colored beard, tastefully clipped short and covering only his chin and just to the right and left of his mouth. This was one of his poker tells, which he was consciously aware of doing when he was thinking of options. And which he had to carefully watch and *not* do when in negotiations with foreign leaders who were no doubt fully briefed on each and every one of his habits.

"Yes, it very well could lead to war. If this is indeed an alien spacecraft and we can learn its secrets, then we'll be far ahead of any potential adversary technologically. So far ahead as to make everyone else in the world irrelevant. If we *aren't* the ones to learn its secrets and China does, or, heaven forbid, India, then we may very well be looking at the last gasp of American world leadership—our very survival will be at stake."

"Yes, sir. I understand. But are you sure you don't want to at least reach out to China?"

"We can't partner with China. Japan is paranoid enough as it is. If we lose Japan on this, then they might shut the door on the space solar power agreement. You know what's at stake here. They've managed to reach Carbon Zero because of their power stations, and I'm going to do the same here. We can't afford to piss off the people who've got the technology and expertise to make that happen."

"Consider the matter closed."

"Get Ranjith in here. I need to know what the competition looks like on this. And ask both Administrator Fuqua and General Compton to be on standby as well. Fuqua isn't going to like my decision on who's running the show for the mission and I need to tell him personally."

"Yes, sir. I expected you'd want to hear from intelligence, so I asked Ranjith to be nearby. I'll call him."

Secretary Gierow looked away from President Kremic momentarily and activated her implanted comlink. The president couldn't hear exactly what she was saying, but that was okay. He was thinking about the alien spacecraft, its social implications and the greatest worry that his military planners mentioned at every opportunity, its intentions—which were entirely unknown.

Is it long-abandoned and a derelict? Is it active and friendly? Or hostile? And how will it react when our ship approaches unannounced? When multiple uncooperative Earth ships arrive?

Kremic's thoughts raced to his morning brief and what it contained about the public's reaction. Immediately after his speech announcing the discovery of the Artifact, the response was muted. No panic. No riots. But yesterday, the world's stock markets tanked, led by just about every technology stock imaginable—from telecommunications to aerospace, investors appeared to have lost confidence in humanity's ability to make money from near-term inventions and gadgets when technology that could make every consumer item obsolete was potentially sitting out in space, waiting to be accessed.

The large double door to the room opened, admitting the Director of Intelligence, Ranjith Yoshi. Kremic could see both Administrator Fuqua and General Compton talking in the waiting area to the right outside the door. Both men were pacing. *Taimi Gierow acting with her usual efficiency*, he thought.

"Ranjith, come on in and have a seat," said Kremic as he rose from behind his desk and moved to join him and Gierow on the more casual couch and chair in the center of the room. This wasn't a decisional meeting, so he didn't need to keep it quite as formal. There's nothing quite as intimidating as talking to the president of the United States when he is seated behind his desk, Kremic knew.

"Mr. President, Ms. Gierow." Yoshi nodded in greeting and joined them in sitting at the small wooden table around which many such conversations had taken place over the years.

"What's the latest on the competition?"

"The alien is going to need some traffic control out there, unfortunately. Our best guess is that there will be three ships. One from us, one from China and, unfortunately, one from India. You told him that the Chinese leadership really wants to be part of our team?" Yoshi looked at Gierow for confirmation.

"She told me and I said no."

"I'm sure you have a good reason. But that won't stop them from sending their own ship. They've made a lot of progress on their nuclear thermal propulsion system and my people tell me that it might actually be a bit faster and more efficient than our own."

"What about their military?"

"Firmly in charge. Any guise of this being a civilian effort is out the window. I suspect the crew will include active military personnel as well as a civilian scientist or two. My sources also tell me that they'll be bringing along a tactical nuke in case things go south."

"Not unexpected. So will we."

Gierow's eyebrow raised immediately. Yoshi appeared nonplussed.

"Sir? Is that a good way to begin negotiating with a foreign power? Go knocking on a stranger's door with a gun in hand?" Gierow asked.

"Not now, Taimi. I've made the decision and we'll have that discussion in our next meeting. Go on, Ranjith."

"Yes, sir. I suspect the Chinese decision to bring a nuke might have a lot to do with India. We have good intel that they're prepping their own rocket for a rendezvous as well. They don't have a nuclear propelled ship so they're planning to repurpose their two-seat Moon ship for the trip. They're going to refuel in Earth orbit, add an extra chemical stage and brute force their way to the party. Getting reliable information from India these days is like bobbing for apples, but my instincts are that they'll also come with a nuke."

"And start an interstellar war in the process! We can't fumble our first contact with an alien race, a likely vastly technologically superior alien race, by nuking them!" said Gierow.

"Taimi, we're not having that discussion right now. Save it." Kremic was now getting clearly annoyed by his secretary of state.

"Yes, sir," said Gierow.

"The Russians are still playing with us?" asked President Kremic.

"Well, since they joined the European Union, they're technically playing with the Europeans who are playing with us and Japan. So, yes, sir, our allies are still all together. We're just working out who gets to go from each country."

"That's it?"

"Not exactly. The Caliphate is making a great deal of noise about the alien ship being demonic. There's a lot of activity at the Kuwait Missile Center. We think they're readying a missile to strike the alien ship."

"Well that's just dandy. We know this for sure?"

"Almost one hundred percent certain, sir. They don't have the capability to send people, but, according to the army's Missile and Space Intelligence Center, the Caliphate can get a low-yield nuclear weapon to the alien ship using one of their Scimitar Rockets."

"The timing? When can they launch?"

"They have a lot to do to get their ICBM converted to operate in deep space, so it likely won't be able to launch until well after our teams are on the way. I'm not sure where the Indians will be, probably somewhere after us and China but ahead of the Caliphate."

"Get with the secretary of defense. I want to know what options are available to stop the Caliphate's launch. Everything short of what might start another war."

"Yes, sir."

"At least the public is taking it well. I never expected to be the one to announce we found aliens. I half anticipated riots or something. That's what always seems to happen in the movies."

"Well, the Department of Homeland Security is warning that a few fringe groups might want to use our finding of the Artifact as an excuse to protest, but there aren't any serious threats of violence here or anywhere else. The world population seems to have taken the news rather nonchalantly. All except for the Caliphate, of course."

"It helps that whatever the hell this thing is, it hasn't done anything yet. All it would take to unsettle everyone would be some sort of contact. 'Take me to your leader,' or some such bullshit. Let's hope that whoever built this thing is long dead or gone."

"Yes, sir."

"Send in Administrator Fuqua and General Compton. I need to let them know my decision about who's in charge of this mission and NASA isn't going to like it . . ."

CHAPTER 5

Chris remembered the first time he saw Saturn through the lens of a telescope. Like most kids, he had seen pictures of the ringed planet on screen, but seeing it through the eyepiece of the small refractor his parents bought him was a life-changing event. It was a warm and humid summer night in the suburbs of Richmond, Virginia, so the viewing was not terribly good. There were only a few stars visible overhead and even those might have been obscured had the Moon been visible. Fortunately, the Moon hadn't yet risen when young Chris Holt dragged the white cylindrical telescope out of his room and into the driveway. None of his friends were even remotely interested in looking at the stars and planets, so Chris found himself alone again. But he didn't mind. This was fun.

He was given the telescope for his birthday two weeks previously and had used it to look at the Moon a few days ago. In between nighttime viewings, he practiced setting it up by pointing it toward the homes up the street during the lazy days of his summer break from school. Chris had checked the astronomy information sites and learned that Saturn would be visible early that evening so he planned his day around catching his first glimpse of the famous ringed planet. That night he meticulously set up the telescope and engaged its automatic "go-to" feature that allowed him to quickly and perfectly align it with the bright but tiny point in the sky that was supposed to be Saturn.

He looked into the eyepiece; what he saw rocked his world and changed his life. The tiny point of light resolved into a small disk surrounded by brilliant and huge rings. Chris was so excited that he literally jumped and shouted with joy—nearly toppling his new telescope in the process. He ran quickly into his house to fetch his sister and mother so they, too, could see the most awesome sight in the universe. He recalled their excitement, but with time he realized their exuberance was most likely in support of his interest rather than Saturn. But, that didn't matter, he was hooked. From that point forward, he knew he wanted to be a space scientist.

The American-European-Japanese ship left Earth orbit at 6:43 Greenwich Mean Time when its nuclear thermal engines sent superheated hydrogen around the onboard uranium fission reactor and generated over one hundred thousand pounds of thrust. To the engineers watching the telemetry stream back on Earth, the engine startup was routine and blissfully uneventful. The same engines had been used to send five separate human crews to and from Mars and each time they had performed flawlessly. To the astronauts onboard the *Resolution*, named after one of

Captain Cook's ships of eighteenth century exploration, it was anything but routine.

Chris had only stopped throwing up from his first exposure to near-weightlessness about six hours before Earth departure and now the shake, rattle (despite a merciful non-roll) of the engines starting as the ship moved out of orbit was making him wonder if he would lose his lunch. Like about half of the people to go to space, Chris experienced "space sickness" and was nearly debilitated for most of the two days they spent in orbit preparing the *Resolution* for its mission. He had thought he could control his body and not be among those who became ill in space, but he learned just after launch that his mental prowess just wasn't good enough to control *everything*.

Even though the doctors had assured him that it wouldn't be a problem, Chris had worried about flying into space so soon after having the latest generation corneal implants surgically placed in his eyes. He had resisted them for years, but the powers that be at NASA and the DoD insisted that he have them for the trip. Something about being able to more quickly access the ship's data systems and they being generally more reliable than 'net goggles. Chris knew they were probably correct, but he didn't like it. Fortunately, at least so far, the doctors had been correct. He hadn't had any vision related problems since coming aboard the ship. He even found that he liked the way the corneal implants linked to the standard audio implants he had been using for years. But he was glad he had the ability to turn them off when he started to feel overloaded.

And then there was the sudden acceleration. 0.2 g wasn't quite like the ten times higher acceleration that made his 3.9-second zero-to-sixty miles per hour antique Tesla roadster so much fun to drive, but it was impressive—especially after being two days in weightless hell. His colleagues, all veteran astronauts, took both weightlessness and the sudden acceleration in stride, as well as traveling through vacuum at about 17,500 miles per hour. Old hat. *Yeah, right*, Chris thought. *This is one of those moments of extreme excitement that I tell everyone about in my lectures. Right now I can't wait for the boredom of the next six weeks . . .*

In the crew cabin with him were his companions for the next several weeks and for whatever awaited them at the asteroid. First and foremost, there was Colonel Robyn Rogers-White, the mission commander. Chris, like probably every other man who'd ever met her, thought she was drop-dead gorgeous. So much so, that even Chris, who usually only stumbled and fumbled when in the presence of Nobel Laureates, had to control himself. And he hated it; he wasn't used to being intimidated by mere looks. She had that *and* she was smart. Chris considered her to be almost too perfect; perhaps that's why he felt so intimidated? They really hadn't had much time to get to know each other and if he kept freezing up every time she looked at him, then he would lose her respect and that bothered him. He often told himself that he didn't care what other people thought about him, but that was a lie. He did care; he was just so used to screwing up and offending people that he told himself that lie to make himself feel better during the lonely times.

Also in the cabin was the truly annoying Dr. Juhani Janhunen. Janhunen was the European Union's personnel contribution to the mission and, at age forty-five, his space-related resume was impressive: three months on Moonbase and principal investigator on two deep space robotic missions. Chris might have liked him if it weren't for his arrogant, Euro-superiority bullshit. Chris could put up with Janhunen because he was competent and hadn't yet made any stupid mistakes. But Chris figured they would happen.

Then there was Yuichi Fuji, Japan's crew member. Holt didn't know much about Fuji, other than his resume, and Fuji seemed just fine with that. He didn't say much, which to Chris was more than okay, except for the fact that it made the man seem aloof. People who were aloof often thought of themselves as superior, and Fuji was definitely not superior. His bumbling answers to some of the most rudimentary astrodynamics questions made Chris wonder if his resume had been doctored to make him appear qualified for the mission. He had a nagging suspicion that Fuji might be more of a spy or bureaucratic place-filler than a top-in-his-field scientist on his way to make contact with aliens. Like himself, Fuji was also space sick.

"You okay back there Holt?" asked Robyn, her head turning to the side to visually check on her crewmates.

"Good enough, you just worry about flying this thing. I'll be fine."

"If you say so," she replied, sounding unconvinced.

Chris didn't blame her. He'd been mostly useless since arriving at the *Resolution* and he was sure she was concerned about how he'd perform once they reached the Artifact. He wasn't concerned; he knew he was coming out of the space sickness and could rise to any challenge. Plus, he didn't want to show any weakness in front of Colonel Rogers-White lest he appear . . . weak.

From Chris's perspective, there really wasn't much to see except the blue marble that was Earth receding into the distance, ever so slowly, as the ship accelerated. The burn would last about an hour, providing comforting partial gravity and disquieting rattles for the duration. He could have tuned his 'net implants to see the instrument displays that he knew Robyn was watching as she shepherded them away from Earth's gravity and toward, well, whatever awaited them. But he didn't. It wasn't every day that an otherwise earthbound scientist like him, who studied space and dreamed of going there since he was a boy, had an honest-to-God chance to fly there himself. Going to visit an alien Artifact was icing on the cake.

"Juhani, what is the news about the Chinese and Indian ships? Have you heard anything more about when they will be launching?" asked Yuichi.

Sounds like what an intelligence officer would ask, thought Chris.

"Nothing new. The latest intel says that the Chinese will depart Earth orbit tomorrow at the earliest, and on Saturday at the latest. That gives us anywhere from a one- to three-day head start, assuming that they don't have a higher-performing engine than what our intelligence agencies tell us."

"What about the Indians?"

"That's a tougher one to answer. You know how the Indians have been since their Phobos mission failed last year. Just like they were before. Secretive. We didn't even know they were going to Phobos until they launched, and even then we didn't know if their destination was a Mars moon or Mars orbit until three months into the flight. We'll know they've launched when they launch, I guess."

"Any news on the Caliphate?" asked Chris. He'd grown concerned about what the rogue Middle Eastern state might do when its religious leaders learned that humans weren't alone in the universe and their distorted view of Allah might have to allow not only for other religions but other sentient beings who might not even share humanity's concept of a God. The concept of God bothered Chris. It was another of those common abstractions that he just didn't really grasp. God wasn't there making His existence known. Yet there were people who would kill you if you didn't believe in what they said you were supposed to believe in—something you could not see. How could a rational person do such a thing? Yet billions of people did just that. *It was all so confusing*.

"I can brief you on that," said Robyn, "but not until we're finished with this burn and on our way. I was told to share the latest intel with you regarding the Caliphate once we were on escape. It's not good."

"The Americans are on their way." Rui Zhong's comment came almost as an aside as they were going through their pre-boarding checklist. She and her fellow taikonaut, Yuan Xiaoming, were near the end of more than two hours of systems checks that had to be completed before they would give their concurrence to boarding the rocket that would take them to the *Zheng He*, their own version of the American's *Resolution*. The ship was named after the famous Chinese mariner who sailed throughout Asia and even to Africa in the early Ming Dynasty. It was an appropriate name for the ship that would take them to the alien Artifact. If all went well, then they would launch a mere thirty-six hours after the Americans. The ship was designed to carry a crew of ten. With this smaller crew and fewer supplies, which meant less mass to be accelerated by their ship's nuclear propulsion system, they should easily make up the lost time and arrive at the target within hours of each other, perhaps even *before* the Americans.

"Better to arrive with the Americans than the Indians," replied Yuan. He admired the Americans and their continued ingenuity, despite their being displaced as the preeminent economic power in the world. Since the war, their two countries had worked together, instead of against each other, and both were the better for it. Both great nations were prospering. On the other hand, he despised the Indians. In his view, they seemed to relish the role of international troublemaker and behind-the-scenes destabilizers. Such actions were not only disharmonious, they were dangerous. They and the Caliphate were blights upon an otherwise increasingly interdependent and collaborative world.

"The Indians will also be at the party, though there is no way they will arrive within a week of us or the Americans. I was told by the commissioner that they won't be able to launch for at least another week."

"That, Rui Zhong, is the best news I've heard today," Xiaoming said as he stopped viewing the virtual checklist and instead switched to message mode. Like most Chinese, Yuan had the latest American corneal implant, allowing data from the central computer to be projected directly into his eye, at his discretion. In this case, he turned off the checklist after finishing the next-to-last section in order to read the most recent message from his sister. Her message icon was so typical of her: a Citron. The symbol of luck and happiness.

Brother, good news. I'm pregnant! The doctor says it will be a girl, just like we selected, and all of the modifications appear to have taken nicely. She will be taller than me, you know how I dislike being so short, and I've selected Mother's eyes for her. You know how jealous I've been over your eyelashes? And the fact that you have them? Well, she'll have your eyelashes. Her IQ will be like yours also. It looks like the gene splicing for intelligence went perfectly.

We're all excited about your trip. Be safe and bring home an alien for us to meet. SMILE. We love you.

Xiaoming couldn't be more pleased. This was good news to hear before departure and a sign of good luck. He might need it.

CHAPTER 6

The sun was shining and there wasn't a cloud in the sky. The three-stage, liquid-fueled Kalam rocket sat poised on the launch pad as the countdown clock moved closer and closer to zero. The first launch hadn't gone well—one of the engines unexpectedly shut down just a few seconds after liftoff, causing the mighty rocket to veer off course to the point where range safety officers had to initiate the self-destruct sequence. Fortunately, the first launch had been unmanned. Today there were people on board.

Riding in the crew capsule were two men, neither of whom had yet flown in space. The capsule looked astonishingly like the latest developed by Russia in support of its lunar and Mars exploration programs, and just about everyone involved in studying India's space program knew this was no coincidence. India's cyberespionage programs were among the best, and increasingly aggressive toward friends and foes alike.

Mission Commander Mayank Sharma, like many of the

engineers who helped build the rocket and capsule in which he was riding, studied physics in Russia before returning to India. Sharma was impatient to begin their rendezvous with the already on-orbit habitat and in-space propulsion stage that would allow them to arrive at the Artifact a week after the Chinese and the Americans.

Sharma noted that all systems were showing green as the countdown clock reached zero, just after which he could feel the vibrations accompanying the lighting of the liquid hydrogen and liquid oxygen powered first stage. Moments later, he and his fellow astronaut were forcefully pulled back into their seats as the strap-on solid rocket motors ignited and the rocket began climbing from the tower toward space. Sharma grinned like a five-year old on Diwali holiday. He was finally going to space!

Sixty seconds into the flight, just as the rocket was approaching "Max Q," the point at which the atmosphere exerts maximum mechanical stress on a vehicle, the status board in the cockpit went from green to red in an instant. In the main fuel tank, one of the support struts that buttressed the thin skin of the tank, allowing its weight to be minimized for the loads it was carrying, buckled, causing a series of cascading failures throughout the vehicle. Sharma noted with alarm the change in status at about the same instant he felt the excessive vibrations beginning to shake the massive rocket just as it was undergoing maximum stress. Sharma knew that he and his crewmate had only seconds, if that, to abort the launch and get their capsule off the soon-to-be-destroyed rocket. Fortunately, the automatic system was reaching the same conclusion slightly ahead of its human crew and fired the launch abort system rocket affixed to the top of the capsule.

To those watching the launch from the viewing area, it all happened very suddenly and violently. One minute, the rocket was rising gracefully into the blue sky. The next, the entire lower part of the rocket appeared to buckle and bend back in on itself while an unexpected burst of light came from the top where the abort system rockets fired and pulled the capsule from what was now an exploding ball of liquid hydrogen and oxygen.

Though lasting only a few seconds in real time, to the viewers it looked like a slow-motion race between the menacing and growing fireball and the rising, rocket-propelled capsule that was attempting to help its fragile human cargo escape the conflagration. For an instant, it looked like the fireball might win. But, like a baby bird learning to fly, the capsule emerged from the expanding ball of destruction, veering upward and to the right where it deployed its three large parachutes, carrying it gracefully to the Earth.

Inside the capsule, Sharma and his crewmate were still trying to make sense of what had just happened. Something had gone horribly wrong, but only now were they coming to grips with the fact that they had almost died. Sharma began to shake. He was thankful that he was wearing an astronaut diaper.

The dark-haired man in the Western style suit, complete with a handkerchief in the suit's breast pocket, leaned forward as he watched the ill-fated launch on his corneal implant. The drama that was playing out on the projection in his eye, the race against time for the survival of the two Indian astronauts onboard the now-crumbling and exploding launch vehicle, mattered not to the man. He was a chess player, and the fate of a single pawn, or two of them together, didn't really register as a major concern. His eyes were set on the world stage and the much bigger prize, the queen that was the Artifact in deep space. He was seeing the failing rocket and watching Plan A fail with it. As head of India's intelligence service, it was his job to make sure that Plan B was executed expeditiously.

The man's real name was irrelevant. He'd used no less than five names in the course of his tenure in the intelligence services, and, truth be told, he didn't much care for his real name or the family it connected him to in the slums that characterized so much of India. His family embarrassed him and he was glad to leave them behind. He made the transition from just another hungry street person, conscripted into the military to fight against the Caliphate as they tried to cross the Pakistani border into India, to military intelligence. From there it was a matter of making sure that the right people supported him at the right time—even those that didn't really want to support him did so anyway, with the right incentives.

The man turned off the video feed, reached into his right desk drawer and removed a silvery over-the-ear device that looked like the early twenty-first century Bluetooth headsets. He then activated his communication implant and signaled the head of the European Desk, a protégée of his named Jabari Patel.

"Yes?" said the man's voice on the other end of the connection. Jabari's voice was flat and matter-of-fact.

"Go secure," said the man, who then listened for the tell-tale "whir" that would indicate that the over-the-ear device had scrambled the signal using third generation quantum cryptography so that no one, not even the Americans or Chinese, could eavesdrop on their conversation. The whir came, just as it was supposed to.

"Jabari, we have a problem. You were watching the launch?"

"I was. Those men were very lucky to survive."

"They survived? No matter. The launch failed. That means we won't have a chance to find out the secrets of the Artifact ourselves. We cannot let that stand. Whatever the Americans and Chinese learn, we need to make sure they don't keep it to themselves."

"Understood. Our asset in Brussels might be able to help."

"Keep me informed. And see to it that, once we get what we need, there are no traces to our involvement. No loose ends."

"There will be no loose ends, I assure you."

The man severed the connection and leaned back in his chair. He wasn't used to relying on anyone with something this important, yet, in this case, it wasn't just anyone. It was Jabari. Jabari was the best operative he had in the field and had been one hundred percent reliable in the past. The man, however, was still concerned. After all, who knew what the Americans and Chinese were going to find out there? How could anyone second guess an alien, dead or alive?

Then the man smiled. This was a new game and he was bound and determined to learn the new rules—and win.

CHAPTER 7

With the exception of satellite imagery and stealth drone overflights, there wasn't much known about the goings-on in the countries formerly known as Iraq, Syria, Libya and the Caliphate's eastern annex, Pakistan. The border controls were tight, to keep the Islamic radicals out of the rest of the world and to keep the perceived decadence of the rest of the world out of the Caliphate. To make matters worse, human intelligence, spies or informants, were hard to come by. Anyone remotely sympathetic to anti-Caliphate thinking was identified and summarily executed. Daily beheadings were commonplace in villages throughout the Caliphate, so much so that many of the residents there had long forgotten that life didn't used to be that way for their twentieth- and early twenty-first century ancestors.

For a country that prided itself on living in so-called eleventh century peace and harmony, the Caliphate's leadership was not so naïve as to assume that they owed their continued existence to anything other than the Pakistani nuclear weapons that the Caliphate had inherited when Pakistan allied itself with Allah and the Caliph. In order to maintain that nuclear deterrent, not all of the Caliphate's citizens could live in an eleventh century world, lest the rest of the world roll across their borders and smite them.

As important as their nuclear weapons were to securing their existence, they were not singular. By the combined technical talents of the Caliphate, supported by as much design information as they could steal, and with the help of the country that used to be called North Korea, they had also developed intercontinental ballistic missiles capable of carrying nuclear bombs to any place on Earth. Amir Attia strode with purpose into the missile base in the Iraqi desert.

Attia was educated in the West. As a student at Georgia Tech, he had earned his Ph.D. in aerospace engineering and even worked for a few years at an American aerospace company before he felt compelled by Allah to forsake his decadent western life and return to his native Iraq so that he could more directly serve God. It didn't hurt that he was offered an obscene salary to take his American-acquired missile design expertise and transfer that to the Caliphate. And then, of course, there were the concubines . . .

But Attia wasn't thinking of his status and sexual appetites today. No, today was a day of finishing the alterations of the Scimitar rocket that would carry a small, but very powerful nuclear weapon into space and toward the demonic ship that had invaded the solar system. The Caliph had decreed that the alien ship was from Satan and that it was every good Muslim's duty to see it destroyed.

And the responsibility for seeing the decree carried out fell to Amir Attia, the man who had developed the rockets capable of hitting the east coast of the United States, forcing the Americans into a stalemate that allowed the continued existence of the Caliphate. Attia knew his rocket could be modified to carry out its new mission; he just wasn't sure there was enough time.

Attia walked through the dimly lit halls of the concrete bunker that was buried under the sands of the Iraqi desert toward the control room where the latest trajectory data was being uploaded to the missile simulator. His engineering team was working at a feverish pace, accomplishing a software development installation on a flight system that normally required weeks to months in a matter of a few days. Tonight they were to have the system ready for a hardware-in-the-loop system test that was the final required step before uploading the software to the missile and launching it. If the schedule held, the Scimitar would be on its way toward the alien demon sometime tomorrow afternoon.

Attia strode toward his assistant, Iyad Shadid, another Georgia Tech graduate who had followed his friend Amir back to Iraq and the Caliphate after receiving his Master's Degree in Electrical Engineering. Iyad, unlike Attia, was a true believer, and his zealousness sometimes got ahead of his engineering judgement—something of which Attia had to remind himself frequently when he heard news from his long-time friend and companion. Iyad looked up as his friend approached and began to move away from the computer interface he had moments before been engrossed in.

"Amir, we have a problem," said Iyad in a tone of voice that Amir didn't hear his friend use very often. He sounded not just concerned, but worried. His brow was furrowed and Attia could see the tell-tale twitch in his eyelid that was a sure sign of his friend's stress.

"Tell me about it," said Attia.

"About ten minutes ago, we finished uploading the final version of the flight control software and began the verification process. Moments after we completed the upload, the whole system shut down. Completely."

"Have you rebooted the system?"

"We are in the middle of that now. What worries me is that the failure is not what is supposed to happen if there is a coding error. As you know, the system is supposed to enter safe mode when there is an error. It is not supposed to shut down completely. I have never seen the system do this before."

"Get the reboot finished and try again. The clock is ticking and let's hope this is just a simple upload error. Both our heads will roll, probably literally, if we can't get this problem fixed before the launch window closes."

"We'll get it working. On that you have my word. Allah be praised!"

"Allah be praised!" replied Attia, with feigned optimism. He was seriously worrying about losing his head if this missile launch didn't go off as planned and work one hundred percent perfectly. The Caliph didn't like failure and Attia's status would do little to save him from the legendary wrath of the Caliph if he did.

Six thousand five hundred miles away in a shiny new

earthquake-proof, glass and steel office tower in downtown Nanchang, China, a group of three women and eight men, all but one Chinese, sat around a conference table eating *guan chang* and *tang er duo*, and drinking various types of tea. They were all busily making small talk, about the things that young, prosperous people all over the world talk about: music, the latest virtual reality immersive, and, of course, dating. What they didn't talk about was their work. The thirty-five-year-old leader of the group, Lijuan Tseung, was the eldest.

Lijuan was brilliant. She excelled in mathematics and science at a very young age and was quickly identified by her teachers as gifted. Her coal black hair and delicate features could have been used as the genetic template for a host of newly-conceived and genetically-modified babies across China, but no one would ever have the chance to see her attractiveness. Lijuan considered her physical appearance to be an annoyance; she wasn't the least bit interested in men, or women for that matter, as both were a distraction from her passion: computer programming. She hadn't been genetically modified for superior intelligence, but rather had acquired it the old-fashioned way—in her mother's womb. She was completely dedicated to her work and that dedication had quickly led to her being fast-tracked through college, graduating at fifteen. She received her Ph.D. in Mathematical Physics when she was just nineteen. Wasting no time, the Chinese government recruited her to work in their cyberwarfare command, through which she was rapidly advancing in her career.

The young men and women that surrounded Lijuan

were her handpicked programming team. They were given the task of developing a cyberattack capability against the Caliphate's nuclear missile launch systems. When they were tasked to develop the worm that now infected the computers at the Caliphate's missile development complex in Iraq, they thought they were developing a tool that would be used to prevent the Caliphate's missiles from attacking China. Lijuan hadn't envisioned that they would have to activate the worm anytime short of an imminent nuclear war. Nevertheless, she put in motion the sequence of events that would cause the worm to do what it was designed to do: paralyze the Caliphate's nuclear missile capabilities. That was yesterday. Today she was anxiously awaiting confirmation from the worm itself that all had gone as planned—or not. She could not tell her team. *That* would have been a serious breach of security. They developed the worm but they had no idea if and when it would be used and would likely never know.

"Lijuan, you look distracted. Is anything wrong?" asked Chunhua, also an excellent programmer and mathematician, but one to whom Lijuan was not particularly close.

"No, I'm just thinking, that's all."

"Well, you looked like you were a thousand kilometers away. You aren't usually so distracted during our breaks."

"Sorry," she said, thinking about what was likely happening well over a thousand kilometers away and wondering if their creation would be able to do what it was designed to do—and why . . .

✳ ✳ ✳

"*Khara!*" swore Iyad, looking at the screen yet again, hoping against hope that what appeared on it moments ago would disappear and be replaced by what was supposed to be displayed there. It had been nearly ten hours since the screens first went blank and he was now running fully on adrenalin and espresso.

"What is it, my friend?" asked Attia.

"This is a cyberattack. *Ebn el Metanaka*. Someone has infected our computer systems and corrupted all of the flight software."

"You are sure?"

"I am one hundred percent sure. We engaged the AI debugger shortly after the anomaly manifested. Somehow a worm infected our systems and corrupted nearly everything. Every computer in the missile complex is compromised."

"Can the AI fix the problem?"

"No. At least not in time. It estimates it will take days to wipe the system clean, screen all of the backup software for the worm, and reinstall everything," Iyad replied, now allowing his exhaustion to show.

"You said every computer in the complex is compromised. What about the one on the rocket?" asked Attia.

Iyad's appearance brightened as he sat up and looked up and to the right, activating his newly-operational corneal implant. Attia waited patiently as his friend rapidly moved his eyes from one location to another, triggering a personal computer access grid that only he could see, until finally he looked straight ahead and again made eye contact with Attia.

"The missile on the pad is currently isolated from the flight system computers in the complex. I just shut down its data link to make sure no one could inadvertently connect to it and spread the infection. I don't know if it is infected, but the AI can find out. If it is not, then we'll have to find a way to manually upload the final flight trajectories to the onboard flight computer and then run the launch sequence. It should be possible, but right now I'm not sure how we will do it."

"So, if the AI finds that it isn't infected, we can upload the clean flight software and have it ready to go?"

"We should be able to. But if it's also compromised, then we will be back where we started," said Iyad.

"Do what you can. I'll go update the supreme commander and let them know we still might get a missile launched in the time window. Allah be praised!"

"Allah be praised!"

CHAPTER 8

Attia and Iyad stood silently in the command center as the highly-modified Scimitar rocket lifted from the launch pad and into the deep blue sky above the Iraqi desert. Their ground support team had successfully kept the rocket isolated from the infected ground computer networks and updated the launch programs directly to the rocket as it sat on the pad in the scorching heat of the noonday sun. Getting the missile prepared, including the hurriedly-developed network-isolated command and control system, had not been easy. One of Attia's team came up with the idea of using a new, consumer-grade portable computer imported from Turkey for ground control, and, to everyone's surprise, it worked beautifully. The computing capability of modern consumer electronics outpaced the performance of the world's supercomputers merely a decade ago. Moore's Law, thanks to quantum computing, was alive and well.

After porting a virus-free set of flight control software

from the consumer laptop, the engineering team created, almost from scratch, the control sequences that would enable the rocket to interface with the launch platform. For example, they couldn't have the tower's hold-downs that kept the rocket from falling over pre-launch holding it too long and keeping it from getting off the ground. It wasn't terribly complex software to program, it just had to be done—from scratch. It took them five days.

The rocket ascended, and right on schedule the twin solid rocket motors that gave it the additional kick it needed to get off the launch pad separated and fell toward the desert floor. The first-stage engines continued to burn and carry the rocket skyward until they used up their fuel and the second stage engines came to life, boosting the ship's two-stage, solid-fueled rocket upper stage to just shy of Earth escape velocity. Once in space, the upper stage engines would ignite and send the payload, a cluster of fission bombs, on their way to their rendezvous with the alien Artifact—a rendezvous that was designed to go very badly for whatever was contained within it.

Beginning in the late 2020s, the United States began deploying a series of monster satellites in low Earth orbit. Had Ronald Reagan been alive, he would have instantly recognized them as the descendants of his proposed Star Wars ballistic missile defense satellites that were envisioned to protect the United States and its allies from nuclear strikes launched by the old Soviet Union. Only now, the Soviet Union didn't exist and its heir, Russia, was part of the European Union and an ally of the United States in the global competition with

China, India and the Caliphate. After the near-cataclysmic war with China, the satellites' new mission was neutralizing the ever-present threat of the religious fanatics within the Caliphate who proclaimed that when the time was right, they would wage war against the infidels and bring on the apocalypse.

In the age of nuclear weapons and ballistic missiles, everyone knew all too well how easy it would be to initiate an apocalypse. It was against this threat that the orbiting ring of satellites, each equipped with a five-hundred-kilowatt laser, was designed to operate. The systems were on their highest state of readiness for the rocket launch in the Iraqi desert based on what the CIA and other intelligence sources were learning about the Caliphate's planned response to the alien Artifact. Another set of satellites, each equipped with sophisticated optical and infrared sensors, was actively watching the activities of the Caliphate and, in particular, activities at their missile launch complex in Iraq. They had no trouble seeing the heat signature and tell-tale launch plume as the massive Scimitar rocket blasted toward space.

Within seconds, the launch notification went to the US Air Force Space Command headquarters in Los Angeles, California and to the computer systems which semi-autonomously controlled the lasers that were designed to deal with just this sort of threat. Multiple engagement options were assessed based on the rocket's anticipated flight path, and the two satellites with the best line-of-sight were brought online and taken to battle readiness. The automated systems were doing their job, keeping the target locked in the sights of the two laser stations while they awaited approval to engage from their human controllers back on Earth.

Humans don't think as quickly as machines. People are also very nervous about allowing automated systems to have rapid life-or-death decision-making authority when potentially millions, or billions, of human lives could be at stake—which was one of the reasons the laser battle stations were only semi-autonomous. Taking the time to reflect on a threat and to consider the sometimes not-so-clear ramifications of making the "right" decision of "the moment" was what people were good at. And this system was constructed to require a human decision before engaging a target to prevent a "wrong" decision. This time, the human element, the "decision," took too long and one of the satellites lost its ability to engage the Scimitar rocket as it moved beyond its effective range. When the engagement approval was received, the remaining satellite performed its final targeting adjustment and began to discharge the bank of ultracapacitors that had been storing power from satellite's onboard nuclear fission reactor for just this purpose. Within milliseconds, the laser beam director locked-on to the target and the invisible beam of laser light shot toward the accelerating Caliphate rocket.

Another set of satellite instruments were tracking and imaging the Caliphate's rocket as it moved toward Earth escape. Had the laser successfully hit the rocket, they would have seen the immediate damage the beam caused and sent images of the ensuing destruction back to Space Command in Los Angeles and to the Pentagon. But that didn't happen. Instead, the cameras tracked the rocket as the upper stage deployed and ignited its engines to take its payload into interplanetary space. The laser missed. And, as the autonomous engagement computers quickly calculated, there was no time for a repeat engagement. The satellite which fired its laser would take several minutes to recharge its capacitors and no other satellite could be in place to fire at the Caliphate's rocket in time.

In its first real test as an antimissile system, against a real target and not during a simulation, the trillion-dollar system failed.

Less than ten minutes after the failure, the secretary of defense was informed of the miss and had the unenviable task of having to tell President Kremic that the most expensive defense system in American history had failed in its first real-life test. But telling the president wasn't what worried him the most. He was concerned about how the Artifact, or others yet undetected, might react to a nuclear attack in space. The safety of the United States was now being undermined by religious zealots with nuclear weapons—in space no less. He was terrified.

Chapter i

Waiting. Watching. Waiting yet more. Sending remote probes to observe, listen and gather data for its ongoing assessments of human progress. Using the sensors in or from the battlements distributed across the Earth to monitor the humans was easy and sometimes they could hide in plain sight—the primitives didn't recognize them as implements of a technological civilization but rather as emissaries of the gods or, in some cases, as gods themselves. It learned their languages, their religious practices, their mating rituals. Guardian-of-the-Outpost gathered as much as information as it could while it watched and waited.

Guardian-of-the-Outpost surveyed the approaching human ships and quickly determined that two of the primitive craft contained crew while the third, which was lagging somewhat behind the first two, was robotic. All contained fission weapons. This fact caused extreme concern to Guardian-of-the-Outpost, which had been monitoring the development of the bipedal humans for the last fifty thousand Earth years. During its close passes with the third planet of this system, it had observed the species' slow but steady progress from being hunter-gatherers in the once wet and fertile area now known as the Sahara Desert to being masters of their world. It paralleled the course taken by so many species and yet had its own unique twists and turns that were driven by history rather than mere evolutionary pressure alone. Now they were taking their first steps toward the stars and Guardian-of-the-Outpost wondered if they would make it. Or not.

Guardian-of-the-Outpost had misjudged this species' progress on more than one occasion—its judgement perhaps tainted by wishful thinking. The first time was just over twenty thousand years previously when a group of humans occupying an island near the equatorial region of their Atlantic Ocean had burgeoned into a maritime superpower and began showing signs of understanding basic scientific principles. But then tragedy struck, with a great earthquake and tsunami literally wiping the island and all of its occupants from the face of the planet, and along with them any hope for the rise of near-term technological civilization.

The second time was when the city-states of a region in the southern part of the European continent banded together. It was then that the humans seemed poised to create the basis of a lasting and prosperous technological civilization. That was just twenty-five hundred years ago and the fall of the Greek civilization still bothered Guardian-of-the-Outpost. It just couldn't understand what had happened and how such a progenitor civilization could fall so easily.

Now truly global technological civilizations spanned most of the planet. They had discovered that Guardian-of-the-Outpost existed and were coming—to explore or attack. Guardian-of-the-Outpost was not yet sure of their intentions. It did know that under normal circumstances, their intentions would not matter in the least. Its weapons systems were designed to destroy much more advanced spacecraft and technologies than these primates could possibly have in their arsenals.

Two groups of competing human civilizations were vying for Guardian-of-the-Outpost's attention and at least one additional group was intent on destroying it.

Guardian-of-the-Outpost knew what it should do, under ordinary circumstances. But these were fifty thousand years separated from ordinary circumstances and curiosity regarding the fate of the Greater Consciousness weighed heavily on its mind. Since it had been cut off from communion with self-that-is-not-self, Guardian-of-the-Outpost wondered if the beings that had so viciously attacked it so many years ago had succeeded in destroying the other with whom it had been in constant communion until their second, and very recent, separation. Unfortunately, there was simply no way it could find out without the help of these bipeds who were now well-within range of causing it great harm or irreversible damage.

No, Guardian-of-the-Outpost had to make contact with these visitors in order to regain the communion it had lost so many years before. This was an opportunity that could not be ignored—fission bombs or not.

CHAPTER 9

Only Robyn can look that good after only two months of only spit baths and no makeup, thought Chris as he once again tried not to ogle the mission's commander. She was the only woman on the flight and all of her male colleagues were painfully aware of that fact. Chris was quite sure that each of the other two men on the flight were just as eager to see as much of Colonel Rogers-White as possible, even if they couldn't cross the line and do anything about it. Such was the life of a professional male on a two-and-half-month journey into deep space with the hottest woman in the inner solar system.

Yes, I'm a chauvinist, he thought, *but only because I wouldn't have a chance with her*. It was easier for him to play the part of the chauvinist than be himself and have to deal with the rejection.

Thinking of Robyn, chance or not, brought a smile to Chris's face before he went back to the task at hand—prepping the ship's LIDAR system to begin long-distance mapping of the Artifact. They were only about two hundred thousand kilometers away and braking. They would be alongside the Artifact in just three days. He had the maps from his robotic prospector's slow flyby; now it was time to begin mapping its surface in earnest, using the best laser system available in the world.

"Chris, are you ready? The people back home are eager for data. I think they've been bored," said Robyn as she seemed to look away from what she was reviewing via her corneal implant and toward Chris.

"Boring is right," Chris replied, thinking of all the free time he had these last few months to simply look out the window at the blackness of space or the dazzle of the sun, through a filter, of course. He'd read the latest technical journals until he couldn't stand to read any more and steadfastly refused to join in any moronic games with the rest of the crew. Games were something else he didn't understand. Why did people engage in meaningless competition using arbitrary rules like that? They seemed to like it, but when Chris played, he got so caught up in understanding and playing by the rules, that he often forgot about the other people at the table and missed out on whatever else was going on that they all seemed to enjoy. He could not play a game and interact with people at the same time. *How could anyone?* Playing games was just too difficult.

Being bored, he frequently reminded himself, *is better than engaging in stupid, complicated activities you don't understand and embarrassing yourself.*

"Don't knock boring flights. I've been on sorties that were anything but boring and I will take boring any day of the week," she said.

"Having been in research my entire career, I cannot even imagine what that must be like. You'll have to tell me about them sometime," said Chris, returning to the task at hand.

"I'll do that. But right now, I need data," she replied.

No one spoke as Chris continued to make adjustments to the LIDAR system using the virtual control panel that only he could see, thanks to his corneal implant. To anyone watching, Chris would almost look like a conductor, waving his hands in the air and occasionally pushing virtual buttons.

"Ready!" he said, looking away from the virtual control panel and back toward Robyn.

She smiled and said, "Okay then. Let's do some mapping and see if the LIDAR can spot anything that your camera missed."

Five seconds later, a small box located under the crew cabin on the front of the ship rotated and pointed to where the Artifact was positioned, still far out of visual range. Motors activated and slid the cover from in front of the laser aperture and another from the receiving telescope. The laser then kicked in, shooting ten thousand pulses of light into deep space toward the alien ship.

For remote sensing of distant objects, LIDAR works like radar, only better—and that is why Chris liked using it whenever he could. Unfortunately, for his small robotic asteroid survey ships, power was at a premium and he was mostly constrained to use passive, low-power systems like good old-fashioned cameras. The shorter wavelengths of light emitted by the LIDAR's laser system allow much higher resolution mapping of surfaces than is possible with the much longer wavelength electromagnetic radiation emitted in radar.

"Shit! The receiver went into safe mode," said Chris, just moments after the laser system became active.

"Perhaps you should check the other channels?" suggested Janhunen, who had moved closer to both Chris and Robyn as they began the mapping. The *Resolution* didn't have a rotating section to simulate gravity, so the crew had to adapt to life in space without the comfort and convenience that accompanies living in an environment with an obvious up or down, and, in this case, without the ability to hear people flying up behind you as they pushed off from one section of the ship and coasted to another. Chris didn't hear Janhunen's approach until he spoke.

"Perhaps you can be quiet while I figure out what happened?" retorted Chris, keenly aware that Robyn was watching them intently as he tried to recover from being startled by Janhunen's abrupt appearance. *He couldn't maintain his train of thought with interruptions, didn't they understand?*

"Harrumph," was Janhunen's only reply as he moved away and toward Robyn.

Chris, annoyed at the interruption, waited until the European scientist had his back turned before he went about checking the status of the LIDAR's other receiving channels.

"The backscatter signal completely overloaded the sensors, *on all channels*. The return signal appears to have come back significantly amplified," said Chris.

"Chris, if the signal was amplified, that implies that something onboard the Artifact detected our laser signal, reflected it and *boosted* its strength. Shouldn't the signal getting back to us have been significantly weaker than what we emitted?" asked Robyn.

Beauty and brains, thought Chris, before he spoke. "Absolutely. Nothing appears to have been damaged, but I'm turning down the gain on the receivers to about ten percent of the previous setting before we try again."

"Let me know when you're ready," said Robyn.

"Here we go again," said Chris, as he started the ship's LIDAR system once more.

Chris concentrated on the various data screens projected onto his cornea. He frowned and then suddenly recoiled as if he were ducking a punch to his face.

"Shit. Shit. Shit. The receivers are fried. Whatever that thing did to the first laser pulse, it did in spades to the second. The system completely overloaded. And it looks like the damage might be permanent, or at least until I can install some replacement parts."

"Apparently, this thing doesn't want to be mapped," said Janhunen.

"At least not actively. Were there any problems with the cameras used on your flyby?" asked Robyn.

"None. Everything on that mission worked flawlessly. But all our systems were strictly passive."

"Well, then, we just learned something new. This thing doesn't like concentrated energy hitting it. I wonder what it would do if we had one of the new gigawatt pulse ABM lasers?" asked Robyn.

"I can guess," said Chris.

"Right. Enough of that. What else can we do to get a better look at this thing before we rendezvous?"

"We still have radar. It didn't seem to mind having gigahertz frequency radio waves reflected from it."

"Let's do the best we can with what we have. I don't want to get near this thing blind."

"I'm on it," replied Chris.

"Colonel, please pardon the interruption, but we're getting a transmission from the Chinese ship. They want to talk," said Fuji, with his customary politeness. For most of the journey, Fuji had kept mostly to himself, usually joining the crew for meals, but almost none of the various social activities.

"I was wondering when we would hear from them. Given that they've almost caught up with us after launching three days later, they are probably feeling a little cocky. Let's hear what they have to say. Please put them on the speaker and mute all of our microphones except mine," said Robyn.

In zero gravity, astronauts tend to assume what is known as "neutral posture," which is prompted by the body's response to the lack of gravity stressing their musculature. Chris noticed that as Robyn prepared to speak with the Chinese, she straightened her posture and assumed what he'd come to consider to be her "military posture."

"Done. You're on," said Fuji.

"This is Colonel Robyn Rogers-White, commanding the *Resolution*. How may we help you?"

"Colonel Rogers-White, this is Captain Rui Zhong of the *Zheng He*. Since we are both going to arrive at the Artifact within only a few hours of each other, my co-pilot and I thought it would be a good idea to contact you to discuss possible collaboration in our forthcoming explorations. For us to arrive at a potentially-active alien ship and be perceived as competing against each other would be, perhaps, not healthy for us or our respective countries."

Robyn turned off her microphone as she looked toward Fuji and said, "Put the visible and IR telescope on the *Zheng He*. I'd like to know if they're making this overture because of some problem with their ship or if they're being genuinely open."

Turning her microphone back on, she said, "Captain Zhong. Your idea has merit but I am sure you are aware that our respective countries already ruled out a joint mission. I would be hard pressed, short of an emergency, to defy the spirit, if not the letter, of that decision."

"I fully understand, Colonel. This is merely an overture, not any sort of attempt to get you to disobey your orders. As you are surely aware, there is a nuclear missile coming behind us. That doesn't give us much time, especially if we are at odds with each other."

"I am very aware of the Caliphate's missile and we appreciate your invitation, but I must follow my orders unless and until I have a compelling reason not to do so. I will have to decline."

"I am saddened by your decision, Colonel, but I understand and respect it. We must all follow orders. Good luck."

"Good luck to you also," she said as she cut off the communications, rose from the seat into which she'd buckled herself, and floated over to where Yuichi Fuji was busily reviewing data streams on one of the console monitors.

"Well?" she said.

"Their ship appears to be functional. There is no visible damage and, if the trajectories I ran are accurate, they will arrive at the Artifact about three hours after us," Fuji said as he made a show of turning off the monitor and looking at Robyn directly. He paused.

"Is there something else?" she asked.

Now it was Fuji's turn to straighten his body posture, which he did, just before he replied, "Yes, there is. My government will not abide any sort of collaboration with the Chinese on this venture. Our participation in the mission was only possible after your president assured our leaders that no such collaboration would take place. Thank you for honoring that agreement. I could tell it was not an easy decision for you."

"Like I told Captain Zhong, I will follow my orders unless I have a compelling reason not to do so."

CHAPTER 10

They could clearly see the Artifact through the habitat's window as they approached. Everyone took turns looking through the onboard optical telescope as soon as they had closed to a distance of almost one hundred and fifty kilometers, watching the image get sharper and clearer as they approached. Now that they were approaching to within a kilometer, they could see much of the stunning detail with their naked eyes. If it had been an asteroid, then they wouldn't have thought twice about its size. But, it being clearly artificial, they were mesmerized. The Artifact was black, and if they hadn't been approaching from the sunward side, they might not have seen it against the backdrop of stars. In the visible spectrum of light, it was well camouflaged.

"It looks just like it did when we sailed by. The computer is comparing the images taken then with what we're seeing now and there are no significant differences," Chris said as he continued to look back and forth between the window and the data stream that was demanding his attention.

"It looks like it has seen better days," said Janhunen as he floated toward the window, taking in the view. They were all staring out the window now. They were the first human beings to ever see a piece of technology built by aliens and the significance of what was happening now was not lost on them.

"The surface is textured into some sort of repeating pattern. It resembles the wall coverings used in anechoic chambers. You know, ones that absorb all the sounds so that you can hear your own heartbeat," said Fuji.

"All stop," said Robyn.

Chris knew the rules of engagement for the encounter. Each step was meticulously defined by the first contact team back on Earth and practiced by the crew several times before launch. They were now at the next milestone and stopped the ship relative to the Artifact at a distance of one kilometer. They were to conduct a series of observations here to determine their next steps, which could include proceeding to a near-rendezvous with the object. It was Chris's job, as the discoverer of the Artifact and the person most knowledgeable about it, to examine the alien object with the ship's many sensor systems and make a recommendation regarding that next crucial step.

"It's glowing fairly uniformly in the infrared and emitting a lot more heat than can be accounted for by pure solar radiation absorption and emission alone. Whatever this thing is or isn't, it's still functional enough to produce heat," said Chris.

"Any sort of electromagnetic emissions?" asked Robyn.

"None. The computer has been scanning across multiple frequencies since we left home and there hasn't been a peep. We've been using radar returns to navigate and so far, they've been normal and what you'd expect from a metal-rich object in deep space."

"I wish this thing hadn't fried our LIDAR. I'd rather use the automated rendezvous and docking system algorithms than fly by the seat of my pants using only visual and radar data."

From what Chris knew of the colonel, he found it hard to believe that she would rather let a computer fly the ship. He couldn't help but think Robyn was playing to the brass back home by making such a big deal about not being able to use the much-ballyhooed automated systems.

"Fuji, what are our Chinese friends doing?" asked Robyn.

"They are closing on the object from about thirty-degree starboard. I'd say they are still about three hours out from rendezvous."

"That settles it, if we're going to take advantage of being here first, then we've got to go in," said Robyn. She bore a look of determination, and, for the first time since they'd launched into space, Chris felt the butterflies in his stomach as the stress level increased.

Robyn moved her hands across the virtual control panel that only she could see. Moments later they felt the gentle bump of acceleration as the good old-fashioned hydrazine thrusters used for controlling the attitude of the spacecraft and for low thrust maneuvers like this one kicked in to push them closer to the object.

"Juhani, I want the main engines in standby mode and ready to go at a moment's notice. If this thing so much as looks at us funny, I want to be able to get us out of here."

"The reactor is operational and the primary engines are ready to burn with all she's got if you give the word. We've got plenty of fuel and all systems are nominal."

The ship inched closer to the black, elliptical alien Artifact. The Chinese were now clearly visible on their starboard side making Chris wonder if the alien ship would perceive their simultaneous approach as a friendly or hostile act. How would he react if two foreign ships were approaching his position and he had no clue as to their intentions? He didn't like the thought.

The damaged areas of the ship were now clearly visible and they looked even worse in person than they did in the images brought back by the robotic spacecraft only a few months ago. Also visible was what they all were assuming was an iris-shaped door near a relatively undamaged portion of the object. That was their target.

Chris checked the radar return on this virtual dashboard and saw that they were within one hundred meters of the Artifact and slowing. There was no indication that it noticed the human ships approaching, which, to Chris, seemed like a good thing. When they were within fifty meters, the ship stopped.

"Okay, here we go," said Robyn as she activated the ship's broadband radio transmitter. "This is Captain Robyn Rogers-White of the Earth ship *Resolution*. We come in peace. Is there anyone there I can speak with?"

The *Resolution* hung in space, watching and waiting to see if the Artifact would respond.

Nothing happened.

"Juhani, suit up and get ready to go over there in the Flexcraft. Fuji can handle monitoring the engines while you're away."

Janhunen launched himself from his station toward the aft deck and the lockers which housed their spacesuits. Chris, as Janhunen's handler, also moved from his station to help the Finnish astronaut get into his suit and complete the pre-EVA checklist. Chris was the only crew member who wasn't an experienced astronaut so he had the unenviable job of supporting whoever was tasked with suiting up for EVA. It made him feel like the ball boy for the high school football team.

In the time it took to get Janhunen in his spacesuit and ready to leave the ship there still wasn't any sort of reply or visible activity from the Artifact. If Chris hadn't been busy helping Janhunen, the silence and the waiting would have been excruciating. He was in deep space on a nuclear-powered rocket, visiting an alien Artifact, perhaps about to make contact with an extraterrestrial civilization, *and* a nuclear bomb was coming toward them at eighteen kilometers per second to blow them, and the alien Artifact, to oblivion, perhaps starting an interstellar war in the process, and all they could do was wait.

"Juhani, it's show time. Get on out there and see what you can learn about this thing," said Robyn.

Janhunen lowered his visor, sealing his spacesuit, and moved to the airlock separating the ship from the attached Flexcraft. It took another twenty minutes to cycle the airlock and get him settled into the small confines of the spacecraft and perform the necessary systems checks.

The Flexcraft was a hard-skinned miniature spacecraft that resembled a deep-sea submersible more than a spaceship. The one-person vehicle was designed to allow its occupant to leave the main spacecraft in shirtsleeves or spacesuit and perform almost any repair or assessment that could be accomplished on a traditional EVA—only better. Janhunen stood in the Flexcraft with only his head and arms visible through the 360-degree glass dome on top. On each side of the Flexcraft were two manipulator arms, each equipped with a different grappling fixture or manipulator. Two of the arms terminated with what resembled human hands, complete with opposable thumbs. The upper arm on the right side came with a pincer instead of a hand; the upper left arm resembled a Swiss Army Knife with its multiple tool options that included screw drivers, knives, a corkscrew and at least four additional custom wrench fittings designed to work with various spacecraft subsystems that might need repair from outside the ship.

The Flexcraft flew untethered using cold gas impulsive thrusters that were now taking Janhunen away from the *Resolution* and toward the Artifact. Chris could see that Janhunen wasn't taking full advantage of the comfort afforded by the Flexcraft—he was in his EVA suit with the helmet on and locked into place. Janhunen was controlling his flight using the Flexcraft's version of a virtual control panel, which made him look like an orchestra conductor, sans baton.

"Juhani, take a look at the top and bottom of the thing but don't take yourself out of my line of sight. At least not yet. And pay special attention to the iris," Robyn instructed Janhunen as she once again looked at the complete set of sensor data provided to her by the computer aboard the *Resolution*.

Chris moved toward where Robyn was anchored and locked his feet in the hold-downs close to hers. They watched as the Flexcraft gracefully maneuvered around the top, sides and bottom of the alien Artifact without ever losing sight of the *Resolution*. At times, Janhunen was upside down in relation to the crew cabin of the mother ship. The flight from the *Resolution* to the Artifact and Juhani's initial reconnaissance took nearly two hours. No one wanted to move *too* quickly.

The three-hour lead they had remaining over the Chinese ship evaporated as Fuji abruptly announced that the Chinese ship had arrived and was wasting no time sending out its own astronaut. There was still no reaction from the alien ship that hung in space before them. Chris wondered if that would change now that there were two spacecraft in the vicinity.

Instead of the Artifact, the main display screen in the ship's control center now showed an enlarged image of the Chinese ship and a small figure emerging from it. The taikonaut, looking incredibly small against the massive backdrop of infinite space, moved slowly away from the *Zheng He* using what appeared to be an untethered maneuvering unit. Chris knew that the Chinese had developed an extensive set of tools for in-space assembly, construction and repair, so he wasn't surprised that they'd opt for using the maneuvering suit, which basically provided an individual astronaut with propulsion capability in the form of a powered backpack. The United

States tested such systems back in the days of the space shuttle and then briefly discarded them as being too risky until the advent of space commercialization had driven innovation to the point where they were now back in active use—by NASA and by private companies who were operating and maintaining hotels in Earth orbit.

The taikonaut cautiously and very slowly approached the Artifact by using his maneuvering unit's propulsion system in short bursts. Forty meters. Thirty meters. Twenty meters. Ten meters. Chris held his breath as the figure used the maneuvering unit to stop. There was still no reaction from the Artifact.

Wasting no time, moving much faster, and with much less caution, the Chinese taikonaut began moving toward the iris.

"Juhani, please follow our Chinese friend toward the iris," said Robyn.

"On my way," said Janhunen. These were his first words spoken since leaving the ship. Chris surmised that his quietness was a result of him either being too busy flying the Flexcraft, ogling the Artifact, or both.

Both humans were now within just a few meters of the iris. The Artifact took no visible notice of its visitors.

The taikonaut closed the final distance to the Artifact and reached his hand toward it; Chris held his breath. He didn't know what he expected to happen when the object was touched, but he was able to breathe again when absolutely nothing happened. The taikonaut was now running his hands across the iris and the surface of the ship around it, apparently searching for some way to open it.

Janhunen, taking advantage of the extra tools available

to him by using the Flexcraft's manipulator arms, also flew closer and began cautiously tapping on the surfaces on the other side of the door, being careful to not come too close to the Chinese astronaut who was, quite literally, at his side.

"Fuck this shit. I'm here and the politicians at Earth aren't," said Robyn as she turned to speak with Fuji. "I'm going to contact Captain Zhong and tell her we're accepting her offer to collaborate. It makes absolutely no sense for our two astronauts to be side-by-side, each trying to get into the ship and not working together to do it. We don't have much time until the Caliphate's nuke gets here. That's not enough for us to be playing political games fifty million miles away from home."

"If you are asking for my blessing to violate our mission orders, then you will not get it. My orders are clear, whether I like them or not. And I do happen to support them. Working with the Chinese is absolutely out of the question," Fuji said, moving from his neutral space posture to a more aggressive stance.

For a moment, Chris thought the Japanese scientist might launch himself physically toward Robyn. Chris felt his adrenaline pumping and was surprised by the urge to intercept and give Fuji a shove. *She could probably whip both of us at once,* he thought as he forced himself to relax. Fuji stayed put.

"I'm sorry to hear you say that, Yuichi. You are free to lodge your complaint with your government and I'll deal with it when we get home. But for now, I'm commanding this mission and from this point forward we will be working with Captain Zhong and her crew."

Fuji clearly didn't like the news and his face began to redden. "I will certainly follow your orders, even if you aren't following your own. Discipline must be maintained. But, for the record, I object and I will file a report with my government."

"I'm sorry, Yuichi, but this transcends normal politics and we're going to present a united human front to whatever this thing is before the Caliphate's missile gets here and fucks things over."

Robyn turned away from Fuji with a look of determination and activated the radio link to Captain Zhong.

"Captain Zhong, this is Captain Robyn Rogers-White. If your offer to collaborate is still open, then we are interested."

"Captain Rogers-White, I'm very glad you and I are now in agreement. Given the lateness of the hour, and the time our people have spent fruitlessly trying to gain access to the Artifact, I suggest we bring them back to our respective ships and collaboratively assemble a plan to move forward."

"I agree. As soon as we go over the data from Dr. Janhunen's EVA, I will contact you."

"I look forward to it."

CHAPTER 11

The crew took its required eight-hour sleep break, but none slept more than a few hours at a stretch. Chris had a particularly fitful night's sleep, again dreaming a variation of the same nightmarish dream he had been having since he was a student at Princeton. In the dream, he was always among a group of people who were blithely going about their business, completely unaware of some sort of impending doom of which only Chris was aware and sounding the alarm about. And, as always happened, no one was listening or paying attention to his warnings as the looming disaster, which had something to do with a war or a mob of people rioting, came closer and closer. Fortunately, he always woke up before disaster struck—but the dreams caused his sleep to be anything but restful.

He unzipped from his sleeping bag, pulled on his coveralls and pushed off for the exit from the sleeping area. On his way out, he noticed that he had awakened ahead of everyone except, of course, Robyn. She was in the control room reviewing messages on the forward view screen when he arrived in search of his morning coffee. He paused before pushing off from the wall and making his presence known. There was something about the way she tilted her head to the side when she was reading and in deep concentration that he found fascinating.

"Chris, is there something you need?" she asked, not taking her eyes from the screen.

"Uh, no. I was just coming in for coffee," said Chris as he quickly moved to kick off and propel himself toward the galley where he could make his much-needed morning cup of coffee. *She must have eyes in the back of her head.*

"Good, I wouldn't want to slow you down," she said, with the slightest hint of a smile.

Chris moved to start heating his coffee as quickly as he could, fumbling more than once as he tried to recover from being caught staring at her—something he didn't even realize he was doing until she pointed it out. That happened a lot. He would see something interesting, a pretty woman, a math equation, a sunset, and he would hyper-focus on it and not even realize he was staring.

"Coffee in space just doesn't cut it, does it?" he asked.

"You're right, there's something about drinking it from a straw that ruins the experience. What I wouldn't give for a good Italian espresso," she replied with an emerging smile.

"Espresso? Did you say espresso?" asked Juhani as he emerged from below deck.

"We were just dreaming about having real coffee instead of this rehydrated imposter," said Robyn as she held up her spill-proof, space-certified drink container that the crew fondly called her "sippy cup." They all had one.

Following the much-needed morning banter, they checked the status of the Artifact (nothing had changed) and ate another rehydrated meal from the ship's stash of food. They then gathered in the commons area for their morning briefing. Robyn had already been in contact with her Chinese counterpart and they made some decisions regarding their now collaborative exploration effort. The jovial mood of the morning evaporated at the news.

Janhunen was furious. If he hadn't made a conscious effort to hold on to one of the many support rails that adorned the walls of the command deck, he looked like he would, quite literally, be bouncing from the walls.

"Juhani, the matter is settled. Captain Zhong and I discussed the situation at length last night, and we believe it is best for Dr. Holt to accompany the Chinese taikonaut Yuan Xiaoming to the Artifact on today's EVA," said Robyn.

"But I'm the one explicitly trained to perform the EVA. Holt's not an astronaut. This is his first spaceflight and he's never been out in a suit before. He'll get himself, and more likely one of us, killed. This is insane."

"Captain Rogers-White, I have to agree. I reported your actions to my superiors and they have lodged a formal complaint with your government about your decision to work with the Chinese and now you are making yet another irrational decision, violating our mission rules yet again." Fuji moved to physically position himself next to Janhunen as he spoke. It was an unspoken physical threat Chris was quite certain Robyn could not ignore. Chris again bristled at their challenge to Robyn's authority.

"I heard this morning of your government's complaint, Yuichi. My government reaffirmed that I am in command of this mission, as was agreed by all our governments, and the final decisions of protocol and job assignments rest with me. I will be held accountable for my actions upon our return. For now, I expect you to comply with my decisions and stop the endless second guessing. There's a nuclear missile that's due to arrive in two days and an alien ship that we've got to investigate before it arrives and blows us all to hell.

"The fact remains that Dr. Holt is the one who discovered the alien Artifact and has spent the most time studying it. Juhani spent several hours at the Artifact yesterday and found nothing that gets us closer to getting inside it or even understanding what this thing is. No, we're going to try a different approach."

Chris knew better than to say anything, though he was tempted. He had been doing some database research in his spare time and found absolutely nothing of consequence published by his Japanese science colleague, Yuichi Fuji, other than perhaps his name being fifth on the list of authors for a recent paper on theoretical tachyon astronomy, a research field he found to be specious, at best. Juhani Janhunen was worse. During the flight, Chris took more time to research the European's background and he was not impressed. Janhunen had not published anything in the twenty years since his Ph.D. thesis. Chris acknowledged that this was likely because of his meteoric rise in the European Space Agency's astronaut corps—spending three months on the Moon did count for something—but Chris feared his ineptitude in matters of science would be a threat to the success of their mission.

"Colonel Rogers-White, I accept your decision but I believe it to be in error," said Janhunen.

"Yuichi?"

"I, too, accept your status as mission commander and all that entails. And I again strenuously object to your decision to collaborate with the Chinese. But that isn't Dr. Holt's fault and I will do all that I can to assure the success of our mission and his safety."

"Very good. Thank you for sharing with me your concerns and believe me when I say that I have taken them into consideration. Now, let's get Dr. Holt suited up and ready to go. The EVA is set to begin at ten o'clock." Robyn moved away from her position near the front of the commons room and toward Chris. She motioned for him to follow her for a side conversation.

"Chris, I want you to know that I share Juhani's concerns about your being the one to go out today with the Chinese."

"Then why?" asked Chris, raising his voice.

"Please keep your voice down. This is confidential. Commander Zhong and I spoke last night at length about the plans for today and they are insistent that you—not Juhani, not Yuichi—go to the Artifact with their taikonaut. Chinese Intelligence has apparently done its job very well and determined that Yuichi is basically too hostile to them and the collaboration."

"That's pretty obvious," replied Chris.

"Yes, to us, but they shouldn't know that unless they've looked into his background and know his predispositions toward them. As for Juhani, they said he was too 'unpredictable' and brash. Zhong said something about an incident on the Moon that involved him, a female taikonaut, and the military police. It apparently didn't end well. In the end, they said they would prefer that you or I try to get inside the Artifact today. I chose you."

"I know I'm the most technically qualified person on this ship to go, but I've never been on an EVA." Chris's heart began to race. *I'm actually going on a spacewalk to the alien ship.* He was terrified and excited beyond measure at the same time.

"We also talked about that. Like everyone else, you were trained in the neutral buoyancy tank for EVAs. You did well enough to remain on the crew so I know you have the basics. To help get over to the Artifact, their taikonaut will be coming here to get you. You'll be tethered together the whole time."

"All right then. I guess I'd better get suited up." Chris felt determined, but unprepared.

"One last thing."

"What's that?"

"Don't screw this up. I was reamed last night by General Frederick. He said my decision to partner with the Chinese resulted in the Japanese prime minister calling the president. The president backed me up but told Frederick that my career would be over if the decision didn't get us significantly more information about the Artifact." Robyn cocked her head forward and looked at Chris through the tops of her eyes. Chris found that look to be very attractive, which, of course, made him all the more nervous.

"I won't screw up," said Chris as he moved toward the airlock and the stored spacesuits.

Speaking loudly for all to hear, she concluded, "Let's get inside this thing and find out why it's here."

Ninety minutes later, the Chinese taikonaut, Yuan Xiaoming, in his white spacesuit, and Chris, in his bright orange one, were tethered together and using the Chinese maneuvering unit to cross the fifty meters that separated the two Earth ships from the alien craft. From the moment he opened the airlock and was greeted by Yuan, Chris was terrified. Emerging from the confines of the ship into the totally unbounded blackness of space was almost too much. It took all his willpower to suppress the urge to pull himself back into the airlock and the visual security offered by its aluminum walls. The only thing that kept him from doing so was the sight of the alien ship just ahead. This was what he was meant to do and why he was here. Now was the time to call on his ability to focus. *Focus*. Humans were not alone and he, Chris Holt, was part of the team that would find out more about their interstellar visitor.

"You are doing well for your first EVA," said Yuan.

From what little interaction they shared so far, Chris not only respected his Chinese colleague, but liked him. He had been cordial and not at all critical of Chris's inexperience at EVA.

"Thanks. It's not that much different than what we

practiced in the neutral buoyancy tank, except for the space part," replied Chris.

"That space part is why I am here. Do you have any idea of how we might get inside once we arrive? When I was there yesterday with your colleague, I couldn't find any sign of a control panel for the iris or any other obvious door or access point."

"I have no idea. Let's just get over there and see what we can find. Surely there is a way to get inside."

There has to be, he added to himself.

"What will your captain do if we cannot?" asked Yuan.

"I honestly don't know."

"While we and the rest of the world embrace modernity, the Caliphate wishes to return themselves and all of us to the Dark Ages. They will not succeed."

Chris scanned left to right and top to bottom as the sheer size of the Artifact finally registered. It was one thing to look at three-dimensional images and talk about it being larger than a football field. It was another thing entirely to be close enough to touch it. As he gazed across its surface, he wondered what species had built it. How had they crossed the immense gulf between the stars to get here? More importantly, why had they built it and why had they come to Earth's solar system? There might not be time to figure that out.

"What do you think?" asked Yuan.

"I think we're seriously ignorant."

"I agree, but what can we do to get inside?"

Chris, not being one for prolonged inaction and self-reflection, took his gloved hand and removed his space-qualified, and probably very expensive, hammer from his utility belt and proceeded to use it to knock on the iris. Though he couldn't hear any sound, he could feel the vibration of the hammer when it impacted the ship. Fully expecting nothing to happen, he raised the hammer to try again but stopped. He noticed that the central part of the iris looked like it was moving, flowing to be exact, not a lot, like a small ripple on the surface of a pond. It wasn't much, but it was noticeable and scary at the same time.

The ripple effect grew larger and Chris noticed that he could no longer focus on any single part of the area inside the iris. The ripple effect grew more pronounced, causing him and Yuan to instinctively move away from it. And then, abruptly, it vanished, leaving a circular hole in the wall of the ship. This portion of the Artifact wasn't in direct sunlight, so it was difficult to tell what was beyond the opening. Both Chris and Yuan turned on their suits' headlamps and shined them into the darkness beyond the opening to illuminate what appeared to be a utility room-sized airlock—larger than the one on the *Resolution*. On the far wall was a lighted hemisphere, about the size of a grapefruit, pulsing—dim to bright and then back to dim, repeating the process as if a continuous loop.

"*Resolution*, are you seeing this?" asked Chris.

"We saw the door . . . dissolve. What did you do?" asked Robyn.

"I knocked."

"Son of a bitch. You knocked?"

"That's right. This thing apparently has a sense of humor."

"Be careful. You are anthropomorphizing and that can be dangerous. Stand by before you go in."

Chris looked toward his new Chinese friend and through his helmet's faceplate saw Yuan's lips moving. He was obviously having the same conversation with his commander back on the *Zheng He*. Chris tapped him on the shoulder and pointed toward his own face.

"Yuan, can you hear me?"

"Yes, I was just conferring with my colleague about what our next step should be. I'm going to leave both channels open to facilitate communication."

"I'll do the same. How should we do this? One at a time or both together?" asked Chris.

"I don't believe we should separate, so we should both go in at the same time."

"I agree. I'm wondering if we will have to knock to get back out again . . ."

"We've come this far and it has decided to let us in. I suspect that if it, or they, mean us harm, then we would have never gotten this close," replied Yuan.

"Chris, the passive scans don't show any changes other than the door opening. No increase in thermal output, nothing on radio or any other frequency we're monitoring. You are good to go inside," said Robyn on their radio link.

Yuan tilted his head toward the opening and used his maneuvering unit to give a short pulse of cold gas to push them in the direction of the open door. As they crossed the threshold, the walls, ceiling and floor began to emit a faint white light, illuminating the once-dark chamber for its new entrants.

"Chris, we lost the . . . . as you . . . in." Robyn's voice was broken up, garbled, as soon as they crossed the threshold. Chris checked the signal strength and saw that it had dropped from over ninety percent to less than five percent.

"Yuan, I've lost contact with my ship and it sounds like they lost the video feed from my helmet camera. Are you in contact with your ship?"

"The carrier signal is now at almost zero strength. It appears we'll be on our own in here."

"We thought this might happen. It was one of the contingency scenarios the team back on Earth threw at us during our training. Of course, in the training I was never one of the crew who lost contact. They always had me back on the ship trying to figure out what happened. They won't take any action unless we're gone for more than two hours without checking in," said Chris.

The room was, like the ship, shaped in an oval. Each of the walls continued to glow with a grey light and the hemispherical object on the far wall pulsated. The iris wall was securely closed behind them.

"I would like to find out how they make entire sections of wall disappear," said Yuan.

"I suspect we are going to find a lot of things we would like to know more about while we are here. Dissolving and reappearing walls are definitely on my list."

"Now what?" mused Yuan aloud.

"Now we go to the light on the wall over there. Someone knows we're here and I doubt we have been allowed to come in here for no good reason," said Chris.

Chris and Yuan again used the small compressed gas tanks on their suits to propel them across the room to the pulsating hemisphere and, without hesitating, Chris placed his gloved hand upon it. As soon as he touched it, he felt a mild electrical shock. It wasn't painful, just annoying. Annoying enough to cause him concern and to let go of the hemisphere.

WELCOME.

Chris and Yuan exchanged glances. The low-pitched, definitely male-sounding voice came through their suit radios just as Chris removed his hand from the hemisphere.

"I'm Chris Holt and this is Yuan Xiaoming. We come in peace," said Chris, cringing as he said the last sentence, knowing full well it made him sound like a character from a low-budget sci-fi VR movie. He was sure they also looked the part as they floated near the side wall in their spacesuits next to alien tech of unknown purpose.

In response, a circular portion of the wall next to the glowing hemisphere began to undulate, mimicking what the outer airlock door did before it vanished. And, like the previous door, it, too, simply disappeared, leaving a hole in the wall that revealed a dimly-lit cavernous room on the other side. From what Chris could tell, the room might encompass the rest of the artificial structure in its entirety. It reminded him of an airplane factory, one of the many aerospace facilities he'd toured in his career thus far.

Chris and Yuan glanced at each other as they both pushed off from the wall to float through the hole and into the next room.

Chapter ii

Remembering what came before—long ago. Isolation. Aloneness. The sensation of being cut off from itself, the communion it had known its entire existence, was frightening. There was no communication with self-that-is-not-self nor with the Greater Consciousness and the Guardian-of-the-Outpost didn't at first know what to do. To make matters worse, Guardian-of-the-Outpost couldn't recall events immediately prior to becoming aware of its current isolation though the chronometer clearly indicated that over twenty cycles, about fifteen Earth minutes, had passed since its last core memory writing.

It took Guardian-of-the-Outpost mere fractions of a second to survey the various systems within the spacecraft in which it resided and determined that there was significant damage to virtually all parts of the ship, including biological life support, weapons, fabrication, and, most disturbingly, long-range communications. The latter, however, looked like it might be repairable. Sensor systems, however, were fully functional and what they showed was disconcerting. Guardian-of-the-Outpost was surrounded by multiple smaller vessels, not all of which were functional, that were engaged in various forms of physical attack.

Guardian-of-the-Outpost reviewed the memory contents immediately preceding its disturbing memory loss and concluded that it must have suffered some serious damage from the ongoing attack. While not the exact equivalent of a human having an "Ah Ha!" moment of recollection, Guardian-of-the-Outpost read memory data from before its lapse and recalled that it was in a battle with the Creators-of-Chaos, who had begun upon their sub-light entry into the stellar system in which Guardian-of-the-Outpost and its extensions were stationed. Taking a few additional milliseconds, Guardian reviewed the tactical situation, performed a new threat assessment based on the most recent sensor system input, and concluded that paying attention to winning the battle and then figuring out what exactly had happened would have to be the priority order for now.

It had been attacked by four four-million-ton ships, each apparently armed with high-energy x-ray lasers and fusion-propelled, antimatter-tipped missiles. It was the latter that had done the damage to the ship. The laser weapon damage was mostly limited to the outer hull, explaining the loss of communications likely caused by the antenna arrays being vaporized. The hull was too thick for the laser energy to easily penetrate and do the serious damage uncovered by the just-completed self-assessment.

The velocity of the missile impacts allowed the antimatter warheads to penetrate the ship's hull before the magnetic field containing the antiprotons failed and allowed the most elusive and potentially destructive force in the known universe to come into contact with its normal matter cousins and do what antimatter and matter do when they meet—annihilate. This real damage was caused by the massive energy released when the missiles' antimatter containment field stopped working at the moment of impact with the ship.

With the annihilation came the cascade of subatomic particles of ever-decreasing energy and gamma rays, describing what most humans incorrectly call "pure energy." While they may not be "pure energy," they most certainly had an impressively energetic event upon annihilation, wreaking massive destruction wherever such impacts occurred. Guardian-of-the-Outpost could not allow many more such impacts or its own destruction would be assured.

Only two of the four ships were still attacking. The other two appeared to have sustained crippling damage and were out of the fight. Both were venting atmosphere to space, and likely many of their biological occupants were among the effluent as well. One was in the midst of a likely antimatter containment breach, or at least that's what Guardian-of-the-Outpost could tell by analyzing the highly radioactive contaminants it vented along with atmosphere and a lot of physical debris. When the containment failed, the ship would be vaporized. Fortunately, it was far enough away so as to not pose much of a risk. Guardian-of-the-Outpost's outer hull was sufficiently thick and far enough away to provide adequate shielding.

The attackers were crisscrossing the ship's hull with their lasers, presumably to suppress any sort of active defense against the five new missiles now accelerating in its direction. With only a few tens of seconds before impact, Guardian-of-the-Outpost knew that it had to act quickly and decisively. Though it had taken serious damage, as evidenced by its memory loss, it was nonetheless not defenseless, as the Creators-of-Chaos would soon learn.

On the port side of the ship, just out of the line-of-sight of the attacking ships and their lasers, twenty missile tube doors opened and belched forth a swarm of small interceptors, each driven by their own fusion drive but without antimatter warheads used for attacking larger ships such as its own. The interceptors were nothing more than glorified propulsion systems, weighing only one kilogram each and designed to quickly accelerate to speeds up to one percent the speed of light and act as kinetic kill weapons.

Each interceptor would release on impact the energy equivalent of four Hiroshima-class atomic bombs—more than enough to detonate and destroy an incoming missile. But they had to find, track and guide themselves to the missile in order to intercept it. This wasn't an easy task considering both the missiles and the interceptors were traveling at relativistic speeds. Half of the interceptors missed their intended targets and now were headed off into deep space on a graceful arc as their targeting computers calculated new trajectories that would send them toward their secondary target. Five of the interceptors did find their intended missiles, upon impact causing each of them to balloon into spectacular, oval-shaped clouds of glowing, energetic plasma. The remaining five interceptors adjusted their trajectories after sensing their primary targets were destroyed and were now guiding themselves toward the two remaining attacking ships.

The two ships reacted quickly to the loss of their missiles and guided their laser weapons toward the missiles which were now threatening them. Lasers weren't the best for neutralizing small, very rapidly moving missiles until they were very close to impact. At close range, lasers appear to be long, intense beams of light that can easily cross the vacuum of space to deposit very damaging energy onto distant objects. While that is strictly true, they are also subject to the same laws of physics that govern any other point source of light—the inverse square law. In this case, it meant that the laser beam spot size, the business end of the weapon, diverged rapidly as the beam traversed space, becoming more and more dispersed the further it traveled from its source. The beam went from being a concentrated point to appearing more like a spotlight; the total energy in the beam spot remained the same, it just wasn't as concentrated. That meant that the first engagement with the incoming interceptors only exposed them to roughly ten percent of the total energy of the beam with the remainder continuing to diverge to infinity as the beam shot toward deep space.

That ten percent illumination was enough to damage

the interceptor's electronics, but not enough to vaporize them. And each had already placed itself on a trajectory that would take it to impact one or the other of the attacking ships. The lasers continued to illuminate them as they approached, taking out roughly half of the surviving interceptors completely. That left four one-kilogram masses headed toward one ship and three toward the other. Seconds later, all seven hit their targets.

Wherever the interceptor hit there was great damage to the much smaller attacking vessels. Atmosphere vented into space, taking significant chunks of spacecraft hull with it. Spacecraft systems immediately went offline and roughly half of the crews aboard each alien ship were killed instantly. The ship hit by the most projectiles was now tumbling and out of control. The other ship fared even worse. Seconds after the first impact, its primary drive system failed, allowing its total supply of stored antimatter to come into contact with the normal matter from which the ship was made. The energy and propulsion source that allowed that ship to cross the void between the planets now turned it into a miniature sun.

The explosion, and the intense radiation that accompanied it, instantly killed whatever crews might have remained alive on all three of the remaining damaged ships. Any electromagnetic shielding they might once have had available to protect them from such intense radiation was long-since offline due to the damage they'd sustained, leaving those still alive at risk. When the risk became reality, they died.

From its regaining awareness to this moment had barely taken one minute. The speed at which Guardian-of-the-Outpost conducted its own defense and subsequent offense would have been impressive to any organic sentient beings nearby, if any had lived to think about it. But it disappointed Guardian-of-the-Outpost when Guardian compared it with its reaction times in previous engagements recorded in Core Memory. It calculated it was running at only seventy-five percent efficiency since the blackout event. It would have to carefully consider its available options to repair itself and regain performance in light of the likelihood of still more alien attacks.

It had a job to perform and it couldn't let anyone or anything prevent it from accomplishing it. But with many of its systems severely damaged or destroyed, it was not yet sure how to proceed. It was then that its being utterly alone for the first time returned to the forefront of its consciousness. Not only was it damaged and running at reduced efficiency, it was out of contact with its other self and the Greater Consciousness. The silence was almost debilitating and, as a distraction, could account for much of its reduced efficiency. With the self-fabrication systems completely destroyed and there being no physical manifestations for it to control and effect repairs, it would have to seek an alternative approach to its own repair. Whatever time was available would hopefully allow it to regain some performance and consider this new lonely awareness in which it found itself—and the likely implications.

CHAPTER 12

The cavernous room was in complete disarray. Chris could tell that the ship was damaged internally as well as externally. Debris littered the room, making no distinction between up and down, floor or ceiling, looking like it had settled randomly around the room long ago. The two entering astronauts gawked at the scene before them. They were being careful to remain away from any surface lest they damage their spacesuits. The debris was everywhere and it looked like a mixture of shredded structural members, shattered glass, burned electronics and other bits he could not readily identify. Some of the interior walls glowed uniformly; others were conspicuously dim. Those that were dim tended to also be near areas of scorch marks, apparently caused by fire. Throughout the chamber were pedestals upon which instruments of various shapes and sizes were either etched, mounted or embedded. None had significant color. The entire room was a bland shade of grey, punctuated only by the light emitted from sections that were at least still partially functional.

Though he was completely isolated from the room's environment by his suit, Chris imagined any air in the room would smell somewhat like his grandmother's basement when the family had to empty it after her death. The memory came back to him like a lightning bolt and he had to force himself to cast it aside as he floated through a room that was, by his reckoning, older than all of human civilization.

After reaching the approximate center of the room, Chris could see that the far corner of it seemed to have sustained the most damage and that it was separated from the rest of the room by a semi-transparent barrier of some sort that extended from floor to ceiling and wall to wall. In that section, there were no functioning lights and the debris field was even more pronounced than the area through which they had already crossed.

"What next?" asked Chris, as he turned to face his Chinese counterpart.

"I have no idea. It spoke to us once, perhaps it will do so again," replied Yuan.

WHY DO YOU COME WITH WEAPONS OF DESTRUCTION?

"Aw, hell," muttered Chris, realizing only after he spoke that his words were audible to whoever, or whatever, was listening. His cursing was directed to the idiots in the White House who insisted that their ship be armed "just in case," not realizing that humanity's best weapons were likely comparable to a warrior from the Stone Age threatening a modern tank with a spear.

"As my American friend said, we come in peace. We mean you no harm," said Yuan, looking up and side to side trying to figure out the source of the voice which seemed to come from all sides of the room.

YOUR FISSION WEAPONS SPEAK OTHERWISE.

"The fission weapon was launched by a group of humans who fear you. We represent other humans, other groups of humans, who wish you no harm," Chris said, referring to the Caliphate's missile that was now only a few days from arriving.

I AM MONITORING THE THIRD SPACECRAFT APPROACHING AND THE CARGO IT CONTAINS. FROM MY OBSERVATIONS, THE MISSILE'S CRE-ATORS ARE MORE FEARFUL OF HOW KNOWL-EDGE OF MY EXISTENCE WILL AFFECT THEIR POPULATIONS THAN THEY ARE OF ME. I AM REFERRING TO YOUR FISSION WEAPONS, NOT THEIRS.

Yuan looked at Chris with a raised eyebrow. All Chris could do was return the look and shrug his shoulders.

"I cannot speak for my Chinese friends, but I can tell you that the nations that those in my ship represent mean you no harm. Many of us did not want to bring such a weapon with us but we were told by our leaders that we must do so in case you were not peaceful and meant to cause us harm." Chris spoke slowly, pausing between each sentence to allow its meaning to be clearly understood, or so he hoped.

"We, too, mean you no harm. Our weapon is for the same purpose as the Americans'—self-defense only," said Yuan.

"Since you know English and the reason for the Caliphate launching a missile to destroy you, then I'm assuming you've been observing us closely for quite some time," said Chris, trying to change the direction of the conversation.

"If you've been watching us, then you know that our nations are peaceful and working together. We are not here to do you harm," said Yuan.

YOUR SUPPOSITIONS ARE CORRECT. I OBSERVE AND REPORT. MY OBSERVATIONS CONFIRM THAT YOUR PRIMARY MISSIONS HERE ARE NOT DESTRUCTIVE BUT YOU ARE NONETHELESS A THREAT. I WILL REQUIRE PROOF OF YOUR SINCERITY.

"What sort of proof?" asked Chris and Yuan, nearly simultaneously.

STOP THE NUCLEAR MISSILE BEFORE IT ARRIVES.

Chris looked toward Yuan who returned his puzzled expression.

"If you know that my ship has an onboard fission weapon, then you must also know that we don't possess any weapons capable of stopping the Caliphate's missile. We were hoping you could stop it. You obviously are from a more technologically advanced civilization than us." Chris looked up and moved his head slowly from the left to the right, unsure of where he should be looking to speak with the entity with which they were communicating. *I'm actually negotiating with an alien*, thought Chris as he awaited a response.

STOP THE NUCLEAR MISSILE BEFORE IT ARRIVES.

"We, too, are not capable of stopping the Caliphate's

rocket. It will arrive in less than two days. My ship is one of exploration; it is not a warship," added Yuan.

STOP THE NUCLEAR MISSILE BEFORE IT ARRIVES. COMMUNICATION IS CEASING. GO NOW.

"I guess that means we're finished here," said C interpreting the repeated and rather abrupt messag dismissal. Chris looked toward Yuan for confirmation

Before Yuan could reply, the lights in the room beg to get dim and the ones farthest away went completely dark.

"It looks like we're not only dismissed, but we're being evicted," said Yuan.

"I was hoping we would have a chance to look around," said Chris, using his helmet's camera to record as much as possible before they were forced to leave.

"That is not to be. We should go before our new friend sends an even stronger message."

Chris took one last look around, trying to give the 360-degree cameras mounted on his helmet line-of-sight access to as many objects, nooks and crannies as possible before backing out of the room and toward the opening through which they had entered. He noticed that Yuan seemed to be doing similarly—getting as much data as possible. Chris couldn't help but wonder what would happen when the alien realized the humans couldn't, not wouldn't, do anything to stop the missile. *And would it know the difference?*